The Cam
Sylvia l

Sylvia Pl
twentietl
remaine
translate
Plath's o
of critic
Sylvia P
poetry, ¡
of key re
scholars
gender (
provide:
written,
explorai

Jo Gill i
Exeter.

The Cambridge Introduction to
Sylvia Plath

JO GILL

CAMBRIDGE
UNIVERSITY PRESS

CAMBRIDGE UNIVERSITY PRESS
Cambridge, New York, Melbourne, Madrid, Cape Town, Singapore, São Paulo, Delhi

Cambridge University Press
The Edinburgh Building, Cambridge CB2 8RU, UK

Published in the United States of America by Cambridge University Press, New York

www.cambridge.org
Information on this title: www.cambridge.org/9780521686952

First published 2008

Printed in the United Kingdom at the University Press, Cambridge

A catalogue record for this publication is available from the British Library

Library of Congress Cataloguing in Publication data
Gill, Jo, 1965–
The Cambridge introduction to Sylvia Plath / Jo Gill.
    p.   cm.
Includes bibliographical references and index.
ISBN 978-0-521-86726-9 (hardback) – ISBN 978-0-521-68695-2 (paperback)
1. Plath, Sylvia – Criticism and interpretation.   2. Women and literature – United States –
History – 20th century.   I. Title.
PS3566.L27Z665   2008
811'.54 – dc22   2008025534

ISBN 978-0-521-86726-9 hardback
ISBN 978-0-521-68695-2 paperback

Contents

Preface

Sylvia Plath is widely recognised as one of the leading figures in twentieth-century literature and culture. Although in her lifetime she published only one collection of poems, *The Colossus*, and one novel, *The Bell Jar*, the posthumous publication of the magnificent poems of *Ariel*, of her edgy and finely crafted stories and sketches, and of her *Letters Home* and *Journals* have consolidated her position as one of her age's most important and influential writers. As Marjorie Perloff puts it: 'This is a body of work quite unprecedented in twentieth-century American poetry.'[1]

From its first appearance, Plath's writing has remained constantly in print on both sides of the Atlantic and in numerous other countries in translated editions. The Plath catalogue continues to expand, with recent unabridged editions of the *Journals* and a new 'restored' edition of *Ariel* offering further material for readers to consider. From the outset, her work has been accompanied by a plethora of scholarly responses and interpretations and each new Plath edition stimulates yet more. The first aim of *The Cambridge Introduction to Sylvia Plath* is to offer new readers an accessible, authoritative and comprehensive guide to Plath's writing. The second is to provide an incisive and insightful overview of key tendencies and developments in Plath criticism. This is an immense and varied field. I have tried in the discussions that follow to offer fair summaries of distinct and valuable perspectives and to present a representative range of critical voices. In my analyses both of the primary work and of the secondary criticism, it has been necessary to be selective. In the case of the latter, the guide to further reading which closes the book offers a list of critical resources that students who wish to continue their studies independently can pursue. In the case of the former, the aim of this *Introduction* has been to cover as wide a range of poems and stories as possible, while reserving sufficient space to address key texts in the detail they deserve. Inevitably, there are poems that this introductory book has not had space to consider or to read as fully as the poems themselves demand. Nevertheless, I hope that the examples, arguments and resources that are included will inform and inspire readers' own further readings and evaluations of a range of additional works.

The Cambridge Introduction to Sylvia Plath begins with an overview of Plath's life and of the literary and historical contexts in which her work was produced and read (Chapters 1 and 2). The next three chapters assess the early poetry, *Ariel* and later poems, and *The Bell Jar* and other prose in some detail. Chapter 6 examines the background and substance of Plath's *Letters Home* and *Journals*, while the final chapter surveys biographies of Plath and provides an analysis of the critical reception of her work.

Inevitably, an *Introduction* such as this owes a debt to the many excellent scholars who have gone before. Their contributions to Plath studies and to my own understanding of the field are acknowledged throughout the book. Finally, this book is intended as an introduction for students and general readers of Plath and is conceived as a supplement to the primary texts. This *Introduction* aims to open out Plath's writing to nuanced and informed interpretation, not to replace a close reading of her own words.

Acknowledgements

Thanks to Ray Ryan, Maartje Scheltens and Libby Willis of Cambridge University Press and to colleagues in the Department of English at the University of Exeter. I have had the privilege at various times of working with Plath scholars Tracy Brain, Tim Kendall and Robin Peel, and I acknowledge the influence of their work here. Final thanks, again, to Neil, Jacob, Freya and Keziah.

Abbreviations and textual note

Unless otherwise indicated, poems discussed in this volume are from Sylvia Plath, *Collected Poems*, ed. Ted Hughes (London: Faber and Faber; New York: Harper & Row, 1981). References to this and other primary sources are to the English editions.

A Rest. Sylvia Plath, *Ariel: The Restored Edition*, ed. Frieda Hughes (London: Faber and Faber, 2004).

Bib Stephen Tabor, *Sylvia Plath: An Analytical Bibliography* (London: Mansell; Westport, CT: Meckler, 1987).

BJ Sylvia Plath, *The Bell Jar* (London: Heinemann, 1963 (under the pseudonym Victoria Lucas); London: Faber and Faber, 1966; New York: Harper & Row, 1971 (as Sylvia Plath)).

BL Ted Hughes, *Birthday Letters* (London: Faber and Faber; New York: Farrar, Straus & Giroux, 1998).

CP Sylvia Plath, *Collected Poems*, ed. Ted Hughes (London: Faber and Faber; New York: Harper & Row, 1981).

J Sylvia Plath, *The Journals of Sylvia Plath: 1950–1962*, ed. Karen V. Kukil (London: Faber and Faber, 2000); *The Unabridged Journals of Sylvia Plath* (New York: Anchor, 2000).

J Abr. Sylvia Plath, *The Journals of Sylvia Plath*, ed. Ted Hughes and Frances McCullough (New York: Dial, 1982) (abridged edition).

JP Sylvia Plath, *Johnny Panic and the Bible of Dreams* (London: Faber and Faber, 1977; New York: Harper & Row, 1979).

LH Sylvia Plath, *Letters Home: Correspondence 1950–1963*, ed. Aurelia Plath (New York: Harper & Row, 1975; London: Faber and Faber, 1976).

LTH Ted Hughes, *Letters of Ted Hughes*, ed. Christopher Reid (London: Faber and Faber, 2007; New York: Farrar, Straus & Giroux, 2008).

PS Peter Orr, ed., *The Poet Speaks: Interviews with Contemporary Poets* (London: Routledge & Kegan Paul, 1966).

WP   Ted Hughes, *Winter Pollen: Occasional Prose*, ed. William Scammell
        (London: Faber and Faber, 1994).
WT   Sylvia Plath, *Winter Trees* (London: Faber and Faber, 1971;
        New York: Harper & Row, 1972).

Life

In the opening line of her engaging essay on Sylvia Plath, critic Sandra M. Gilbert explains, 'Though I never met Sylvia Plath, I can honestly say that I have known her most of my life.'[1] The familiarity that Gilbert reports is one that many readers of Plath share. The bare facts of her life come to us from multiple sources – from her *Journals* and *Letters Home*, her stories and prose essays, her novel, *The Bell Jar*, and of course from the poems themselves. Beyond this, we pick up clues and information from biographies and memoirs, from critical commentaries and, of late, from other people's poems (notably Ted Hughes's 1998 *Birthday Letters*) or fiction (Kate Moses's 2003 *Wintering*) or film (Christine Jeffs's 2003 *Sylvia*). From these fragments we construct what we believe to be the biographical truth. We learn something, too, from the broader cultural, historical and ideological circumstances in which Plath lived and wrote; as Stan Smith puts it, 'For Sylvia Plath . . . identity itself is the primary historical datum: the self is a secretion of history.'[2]

Plath's life, then, seems overdetermined. It is told to us over and over again (indeed, she tells it to herself over and over again, rehearsing certain moments in multiple genres) in so many overlapping layers that it seems, finally, to form a kind of carapace – a papier-mâché shell which masks a gap. Biographical accounts of Plath's life have, as Chapters 6 and 7 will show, been bitterly contested. Nevertheless, it is useful to begin by at least sketching the bare bones of Plath's life and times in order the better to situate her work in its personal, literary and historical contexts. This also helps us to understand the pressures which brought it into being and which have shaped its reception.

Family

Plath described herself as first-generation American on her father's side and third-generation on that of her mother (*PS* 169). Her father, Otto Emil Plath, was born in around 1885 in Grabow, a town on the Polish/German border (or in the Polish Corridor, as it was then known). His parents were German, but one of his grandmothers was said to have been Polish. As a child, he developed a fascination for bees. He excelled at school and when his grandparents, who had emigrated to the USA earlier in the nineteenth century, learnt of his promise, they sent for him to join them. Otto Plath travelled to the USA in 1901 at the age of 16. He worked in New York for a year, earning a living in his uncle's grocery store and sitting in on lessons in a local school in order to learn English (*LH* 8). His grandparents had settled on a farm in Wisconsin and were determined that their grandson should earn a place at the state's Northwestern College. They had aspirations for Otto to train for the Lutheran ministry but he did not share their ambitions. At the Lutheran seminary he became disenchanted with his fellow students and was dismayed to find that the works of Charles Darwin were banned (*LH* 9). He was subsequently cut off from his family. After studying at several universities throughout the USA, he became a university professor and an expert in entomology, specialising in the study of bees. His doctoral thesis, *Bumblebees and their Ways*, was submitted to Harvard University in 1928 and eventually published in 1934.[3]

It was while working as a professor at Boston University that Otto met Aurelia Schober. Aurelia was the daughter of a German-speaking Austrian family who had emigrated to the USA earlier in the nineteenth century. She was his junior by two decades and a graduate student in his Middle High German class. Aurelia's family had expected their daughter to acquire a vocational education and she obeyed by following a business curriculum at the Boston University of Practical Arts and Letters, though she also fitted in additional courses in literature and history and worked simultaneously in secretarial, library and other roles. On graduation Aurelia worked for several years as a teacher and then returned to university to study for an MA. There she met Otto Plath and in January 1932, after a two-year courtship during which Aurelia taught high school English and German, they married. Otto had first to seek a divorce from his previous wife, Lydia, from whom he had separated some thirteen years earlier. Comments made by Aurelia in the memoir with which she opens *Letters Home* (the selection of Plath's letters which she edited for publication in 1976) indicate a mismatch between her expectations of married life and those of her husband. She was a generation younger than him and was accustomed to a degree of independence. His expectations, she intimates, were that she would play a more passive and domestic role (*LH* 5–10).

The Plath's first child, Sylvia, was born at the Robinson Memorial Hospital, Boston, on 27 October 1932. Their second, Warren, was born exactly two and a half years later.[4] At this time the Plaths were living in Jamaica Plains, a suburb of Boston. In preparation for Warren's birth, Sylvia was sent to her maternal grandparents' home at Point Shirley on the Massachusetts coast. She recalls this experience in the prose memoir 'Ocean 1212-W' (*JP* 117–24). In 1936 the family moved to the coastal suburb of Winthrop, close to the Schober grandparents at Point Shirley (*LH* 13–18). Warren was often ill as a young child, thus Sylvia spent much time at the Point Shirley home. The short story 'Among the Bumblebees' looks back to this period, albeit with a fictionalised subject, Alice, and the rather telling conflation of father and grandfather figure (*JP* 259ff; see also *CP* 110). Shortly after Warren's birth, Otto's health began to decline. Apparently fearing that he had cancer, Otto refused to consult medical experts until a minor accident in the home in August 1940 forced him to seek advice. He was diagnosed with advanced diabetes which required urgent amputation of one leg. However, the operation did not halt the progression of the disease and in November of that year he died (*LH* 22–4). Sylvia was eight. A number of poems (most famously 'Daddy', 'The Colossus' and 'Full Fathom Five') reflect on this time as do entries in Plath's *Journal* – for example, one of 15 June 1951 where Plath ponders the biological, emotional and intellectual legacy of her father's death (*J* 64–5). Subsequent entries, particularly those which record her psychotherapy sessions with Dr Ruth Barnhouse Beuscher in late 1958, analyse the trauma of this period in rather more detail and with acerbic frankness (*J* 429–30). In recalling her relationship with her father, Plath inevitably also assesses her complicated relationship with her mother. Aurelia was, by all accounts, devoted to her children and to giving them every possible opportunity, even if this came at the price of her own exhaustive labours and personal sacrifice. The debt Sylvia owed to her mother and to subsequent mentors was one she felt acutely and referenced on numerous occasions.

In 1942 the family moved to a small 'white frame' house in Wellesley, a suburb west of Boston which promised good schools, lower taxes and the possibility in time to come of a scholarship for Sylvia at the highly regarded Wellesley College. Money was a pressing issue for the family. As Sylvia was later to note, her father did not have a pension – a source of deep bitterness to her mother – and the costs of his illness and funeral had exhausted any spare savings (*LH* 29). The critic Louis Simpson has suggested that their new home was an inauspicious place for a poet to begin to write: 'a white frame house is particularly dispiriting, antiseptic and antipoetic'.[5] However, as we will see later, Plath and others of her peers (Anne Sexton and Maxine Kumin, for instance) were to put this peculiar suburban and domestic locale to good use in their work, creating in Plath's case a compelling, if sometimes dystopian, view of modern life.

Sylvia was a high-achieving A-grade student throughout her school career, first at the Marshall Livingston Grammar School and then at the Gamaliel

Bradford Senior High. Simpson reports that one of her teachers remembered her as 'the kind of student who turns up wanting to know why she has received an "A minus" instead of an "A." '[6] In addition to her wide-ranging academic strengths, she was an accomplished artist (at one time she considered art as her future career and her poetry is often influenced by painting and sculpture), a burgeoning poet and novelist and an inveterate diarist (*LH* 30–1). Her earliest childhood publications are poems published in the early 1940s – in the *Boston Herald* of 10 August 1941 and the *Phillipian* (the newspaper of the local Phillips Academy, Andover) in 1945 and 1946. Sylvia also co-edited her high school newspaper, *The Bradford* (*Bib* 102–3). She achieved her first major publication in August 1950 when after countless rejections her first story, 'And Summer Will Not Come Again', was published in *Seventeen* magazine. Her persistence in sending out manuscripts in spite of rejections (her mother mentions forty-five from *Seventeen* before its first acceptance) is one of her hallmarks, as is a willingness, perhaps born of this experience, to research her markets carefully and to tailor her submissions appropriately (*LH* 35).[7] The summers of Sylvia's high school and college years were spent in various temporary jobs includ-ing waitressing, babysitting and farm work, and in frantic dating. These were all experiences that Sylvia relished because they provided settings, plots and characters which she could use in her writing – 'dismembered or otherwise' as Aurelia recalls her daughter commenting (*LH* 37).

In 1950 Sylvia won a place at the prestigious Smith College, Northampton. This was a fraught time for her; it represented the achievement of her own and her mother's dreams (in her early letters home from Smith, she repeatedly declares her shock and delight at becoming a 'Smith girl' (*LH* 46, 48)), yet it also heralded a prolonged period of anxious self-examination. Fellow student Nancy Hunter Steiner describes the 'almost savage industriousness – a clenched-teeth determination to succeed' – that characterised the Smith students.[8] Sylvia may have felt this pressure more than most because her studies were funded by a package of grants and awards which included a contribution from Olive Higgins Prouty, a well-known novelist of the time (she emerges as Philomena Guinea in *The Bell Jar*). She was intensely hardworking and intensely concerned about her ability to make an academic and social success of her Smith years. Her *Journal* entries indicate that she made huge demands of herself, was involved in energy-sapping extracurricular activities, worried about her grades in the Sciences (which threatened her 'A' averages) and about her emotional and financial obligations.

In trying to understand Plath's experience as a young woman at Smith, we need to be alert both to the specific and personal pressures she was under and to the ideologies of the period, in particular how these defined success as a student and as a young woman. She was ambivalent about her relationships with the succession of boys she dated, probably the most significant of which were Dick Norton, a model for Buddy Willard in *The Bell Jar*, and Gordon Lameyer, a student of English at nearby Amherst College.[9] Her letters and entries in the *Journals* from throughout this period trace the pressure on young women to date but to remain chaste, to study hard and to play hard (*LH* 45, 49, 52; *J* 28). Robin Peel suggests that during her years at Smith, Plath's immediate and 'constant' goal was one of 'self-improvement'. As he says, 'the focus on self-development and achievement itself reflects the dominant American ideology of the period. Plath imbibed this so deeply that "success or death" became the rhetorical options to which this ideology was reduced.'[10] We will return to these broader cultural pressures in the next chapter. For now, though, it is useful to point out the peculiar contradictions of life for bright young women in 1950s America.

This was immediately before the rise of what became known as 'second wave' feminism (and a decade before the publication of Betty Friedan's groundbreaking *The Feminist Mystique* (1963)). Women were faced with contradictory and seemingly irreconcilable demands to be both clever and attractive, confident and submissive; to be high achievers yet to recognise that their greatest achievements would be marriage, children and home. Aurelia notes that during her daughter's high school years, she (Sylvia) was aware of 'the prejudice boys built up among themselves about "brainy" girls' (*LH* 38). Plath returns to and wrestles with these expectations again and again in her *Journals* and in *The Bell Jar*, where the impossibility of the choices available to women such as her heroine Esther Greenwood are exposed to dreadful effect. A friend from Plath's later years in Cambridge recalls that after her secret marriage to Ted Hughes, she exclaimed, ' "Jane, you can't imagine what a relief it is to be free of that dreadful social pressure." '[11]

Throughout her early years at Smith College, Sylvia continued to write and to take on editorial responsibilities, for example, the editorship of the *Smith Review* (*LH* 100). She won a $500 prize in 1952 in *Mademoiselle* magazine's national college fiction competition (*J* 108, 679) and in the following year was awarded one of twenty prestigious guest editorships for the college issue of the magazine. In June 1953 she travelled to New York and, with the other guest editors, experienced a month-long internship. Laurie Levy's memoir 'Outside the Bell Jar' captures something of the excitement and the intensity of this adventure for the young women involved:

> By plane and train, from coastal cities and dusty inland towns, we
> crossed the Rockies, the Mason-Dixon, and the Mississippi.

> Twenty – count 'em, twenty – from urban universities and the towers of
> academia and many a Babbittville campus thick with the rotting lilacs of
> that fruitful May . . . we marched twenty abreast from the hotel for
> women on glamorous Lexington to the office on glamorous Madison.
> We whispered in awesome places atop pastel carpets thick as cream
> cheese, our palms and upper lips sodden: each too self-immobilized to
> involve herself in the others' worlds, yet eager to submerge identity by
> joining the group.[12]

The experience and its aftermath are fictionalised in *The Bell Jar*. On her
return home to Wellesley from this month in New York, Sylvia was met with
the news that she had been unsuccessful in her application for a place on a high-
level creative writing course, run by the short story writer Frank O'Connor.
According to her mother, Sylvia blanched visibly at the news (*LH* 123). This,
coupled with emotional and physical exhaustion, and the prospect of a long
and fruitless summer at home in the Boston suburbs, seems to have been the
final catalyst for a psychological breakdown. The few journal entries for this
period (only two for July 1953) record Sylvia's sense of confusion, frustration
and horror at what she seems to have recognised as an incipient mental crisis
(*J* 185–6). In August she attempted suicide by taking an overdose of pills. Alex
Beam glosses the situation thus:

> Trapped at home . . . drained of energy, she began to contemplate
> suicide. After a half-serious attempt to drown herself, Plath hid in a
> crawl space underneath her family's house and swallowed an overdose of
> sleeping pills. She very nearly died. ("BEAUTIFUL SMITH GIRL
> MISSING AT WELLESLEY" and "TOP RANKING STUDENT AT
> SMITH MISSING FROM WELLESLEY HOME" were two of the
> front-page headlines in the Boston papers.)[13]

Sylvia was hospitalised at McLean Hospital, on the edge of Boston (subsequently regarded as the 'hospital of choice' for creative artists; Robert Lowell
and Sexton were to follow Plath in spending time there). Beam explains that she
was under the care of Dr Ruth Beuscher – the Dr Nolan of *The Bell Jar* – who,
after conventional therapies such as the prescription of Thorazine failed to make
any improvement, proposed ECT (electroconvulsive or 'shock' therapy). This
was applied in December 1953 and by the New Year she had shown sufficient
improvement to be able to return to college in time to register for the second
semester of that academic year. Back at Smith she began reading for her hon-
ors thesis, 'The Magic Mirror: A Study of the Double in Two of Dostoevsky's
Novels', which she was to submit the following year. Alongside Dostoevsky,
Sylvia was reading Erich Fromm, Karl Jung, Friedrich Nietzsche, Karl Marx,

Henry James, Sherwood Anderson, Nathaniel Hawthorne, Theodore Dreiser and others.[14] During this time, she developed a relationship with a Yale student, Richard Sassoon.[15]

On her graduation in 1955, Sylvia travelled on a Fulbright Scholarship to Newnham College, Cambridge University. There she studied philosophy, attended lectures on modern literature and immersed herself in student activities, taking part in several plays and modelling the season's fashions for the May 1956 edition of *Varsity* (*LH* 183–203). Her Cambridge tutor, Dorothea Krook, speaks warmly of Sylvia's engagement with the works of Plato – the subject of their regular tutorials.[16] Fellow American student Jane Kopp describes the cultural confusions which arose (and which Sylvia, she suggests, provoked) during their early weeks in England. The differences between English and American habits, tastes and social manners were to become a recurring concern to Plath (see, for example, the poems 'Eavesdropper', 'Tour' and 'Leaving Early' and the sketch 'Snow Blitz' (*JP* 125–33)). During her first Christmas break from university, she travelled to Paris and the South of France with Richard Sassoon, who was then studying at the Sorbonne.[17]

Marriage

It was in February 1956 at the launch party for a short-lived literary magazine, the *St Botolph's Review*, that Sylvia met her future husband, the poet Ted Hughes. Her detailed entries in the *Journals* (*J* 211ff), several poems (for example 'Pursuit') and Hughes's poem 'St Botolph's' (*BL* 14) evoke this period. Hughes was born in Yorkshire in 1930, educated at Mexborough Grammar School and then Pembroke College, Cambridge. He had graduated from Cambridge two years before meeting Sylvia and was working as a reader for a film company in London, though he returned to Cambridge frequently to meet friends and fellow writers.[18] Plath and Hughes married in London just four months later on 16 June 1956 (the 'Bloomsday' of James Joyce's *Ulysses*), then honeymooned in Benidorm (see the poems 'Fiesta Melons' and 'The Goring' and the story 'That Widow Mangada') before returning to Cambridge and London to study and write. The marriage had, at first, to be kept secret from Cambridge and Fulbright authorities as Sylvia feared losing her scholarship if it became known. When news did leak out, the authorities proved willing to give special dispensation.[19] Sylvia then left college accommodation and the couple rented a flat in Eltisley Road, Cambridge. During the late summer of 1956, they made brief visits to Hughes's family in Yorkshire. The growing influence of an English literary tradition, stimulated in part by these visits, is recorded in poems such as 'Wuthering Heights' and 'Hardcastle Crags'. From 1956 to 1957 Sylvia continued her Fulbright scholarship while Ted taught in a local school. Both poets were successful in publishing stories and poems (since 1954, Plath had been placing poems and stories in major publications such as *Harper's Magazine* and *Atlantic Monthly*). In the spring of 1957 – to Plath's particular delight, for it was she who had sent out the manuscript for consideration – Hughes learnt that his first book of poems, *The Hawk in the Rain*, had been awarded the New York Poetry Center Award and publishing contracts with Faber and Faber and Harper & Row (*LH* 297).

Later that year, they sailed for the USA and after a brief holiday on Cape Cod, settled down to a year of writing and teaching (Plath back at Smith College and Hughes at the University of Massachusetts). Plath's *Journals* indicate a degree of ambivalence about this new role. On the one hand, it was an honour to be included among the faculty of such an esteemed institution, on the other, Plath had no female role models who could persuade her of the feasibility in these circumstances of reconciling all her other aspirations. The Smith faculty were largely single (and apparently less than enthusiastic about their star pupil's hurried marriage) and dedicated to their academic lives. Plath wanted, as her *Journals* repeatedly make clear, to write, to teach and to be a fulfilled wife and mother. This route, she feared, might be closed to her in the path she had taken. Kopp recalls a letter from Plath which confirms the apparent impossibility of her position. The letter emphasised

> how odd she felt returning to Smith campus, like 'a rather antique and fallen angel.' It seemed tinged with rue and suggested that she found it difficult to write while buried under academic chores, although there was also a sense of coming of age and a genuine delight in teaching 'very intelligent' and 'eager' girls, especially in such an ideal setting.[20]

Plath did indeed find the contradictory demands of the roles of teacher and creative writer exhausting; by 1958, the couple had taken the decision to resign from their academic posts and try for one year to succeed as writers, earning a living from prizes, reviewing and royalties. They rented a flat on Boston's Beacon Hill and to supplement their earnings from writing, Plath worked part-time in various clerical roles, including one at the Massachusetts General Hospital (the title story of *Johnny Panic and the Bible of Dreams* originated there). She also audited Robert Lowell's Boston University poetry class alongside Sexton, Kumin and George Starbuck (*J* 471). Although this group met for only a few months, it proved of lasting mutual influence. Plath was later to credit Sexton with showing her how to break through to the 'taboo' subjects of her own experience (*PS* 167–8). In an affectionate memoir Sexton recalls the group's routine of participating in the workshop and then adjourning to the Ritz Hotel for cocktails and conversation: 'Often, very often, Sylvia and I would talk at length about our first suicides; at length, in detail and in depth between the free potato chips.'[21] Plath's recollections of these episodes are less enthusiastic. Sexton and Starbuck had entered into an affair, and the former's apparent success both as a poet and as a seductive woman seems to have hit Plath hard at a time when she was trying to revise some of her own poems for submission to the publisher which had just accepted Sexton's first volume. She complained that Sexton was ahead of her: 'with her lover GS writing New Yorker odes to her and both of them together: felt our triple martini afternoons at the Ritz breaking up' (*J* 480; see also *J* 498).

During this period, Plath reentered therapy with her McLean doctor, Ruth Beuscher. She was reading widely in psychoanalytical literature at the same time, and her *Journals* show her working hard to forge a meaningful narrative from difficult childhood experiences and complex adult relationships (*J* 429 ff). In spring 1959 she visited her father's grave at Winthrop cemetery for the first time (*J* 473), an experience which was to inform the poem 'Electra on Azalea Path', completed two weeks after her visit, and to reemerge in fictionalised form in *The Bell Jar*. The early summer was a productive one for Plath: she wrote a number of stories and some of the poems which were later to form the bulk of *The Colossus* (*J* 486) and she also seems to have begun work on a novel, *Falcon Yard*. But there were also disappointments and rejections.[22] Throughout this period, she was trying to become pregnant and this preoccupation underpins much of her writing at this time (*J* 500). Later that summer, Plath and Hughes travelled across the USA, visiting California and Yellowstone National Park, among other places. The story 'The Fifty-Ninth Bear' (*JP* 94–105) dramatises one incident from this expedition (Plath's letter to her mother describes the same scene (*LH* 349–50)). Tracy Brain uses this incident as an example of some of the limitations of biography, establishing that contrary to subsequent accounts of the episode which inspired the story, 'there was no human fatality from any bear in Yellowstone Park in 1959'.[23] The autumn of 1959 was spent at the Yaddo Writers' Colony in Saratoga Springs, New York, where many of the poems from Plath's first book, *The Colossus*, were conceived. By this time, Plath knew that she was pregnant at last. Grace Schulman (a writer who stayed at Yaddo in the early 1970s) regards Plath's time at Yaddo as a period for recuperation and rebirth and sees this process reflected in poems such as 'The Stones' (the closing poem in the 'Poem for a Birthday' sequence). Here, she says, 'the speaker is one who has lived in fragments and is now reborn.'[24]

England

The couple left the USA that winter in order to return to England in anticipation of the birth of their first child. Back in London in the spring of 1960, Plath secured a British publisher for *The Colossus*. This was her first collection of poems, one she had been working on intermittently for at least four years (*J* 294). The move to Britain had given her the impetus to start seeking a home for the collection once more. An editor at the London publisher Heinemann had seen some of Plath's poems in the *London Magazine* and invited her to submit a manuscript – a gesture that Plath read as an omen of great things to come: 'England offers new comforts', as she exclaimed in her diary (*J* 521). The book was published later that year, in October. In April, Plath gave birth to her first baby, Frieda (*LH* 373). Just a few weeks afterwards, she and Hughes met T. S. Eliot at a Faber and Faber reception and attended one of the first Aldermaston 'Ban the Bomb' marches (*LH* 379, 378). The Faber and Faber event is indicative of Plath's proud sense that she was forging links with an important literary tradition; her *Letters Home* of this period recall her acquaintance with a number of influential critics, editors and writers. Witnessing the 'Ban the Bomb' march (with Frieda in a carry-cot) as it entered London indicates her increasing concerns about politics and the environment. As the marchers came into view, she expresses pride that her daughter's 'first real adventure should be as a protest against the insanity of world-annihilation' (*LH* 378). Both poets continued to write – for magazines and journals, for the BBC and for their next collections of poems – juggling space in their cramped London flat, and negotiating time away from domestic and childcare duties as best they could. Al Alvarez, an acquaintance at the time and later responsible for publishing some of Plath's late poems in the immediate aftermath of her death, recalls the scene: 'A typewriter stood on a little table by the window, and they took turns at it, each working shifts while the other minded the baby. At night they cleared it away to make room for the child's cot.'[25]

Plath became pregnant again in early 1961, but in February the pregnancy miscarried and she was subsequently hospitalised for appendicitis (see *J* 599ff and the poems 'Parliament Hill Fields', 'In Plaster' and 'Tulips'). In the months after her operation, she worked on the first draft of *The Bell Jar* (though the germ of the plot is recorded in a notebook entry of 28 December 1958 (*J* 452)). Later that year, desperate for more room and for a break from the financial pressures of living in London and for time to write, she and Hughes bought a large dilapidated thatched house in the Devon village of North Tawton (*LTH* 515–24). They moved in at the very end of August 1961. Plath gave birth there at the beginning of 1962 to her second child, Nicholas. Her *Letters Home*, short stories and sketches ('Mothers' and 'Rose and Percy B') and her entries in the 1962 *Journals* give some insight into the contradictory feelings which her move to Devon stimulated, both as an American in an alien landscape and community and as a poet trying to combine writing, childcare and the management of the home. To her mother, Plath wrote generally positive and chatty letters, enthusing about the house and the neighbours (*LH* 428). In her private sketches, appended to her *Journals*, and in the *Journals* themselves, she paints a different picture, despairing at the constant interruptions, the strange manners of the locals and the pressures to conform to village life. At this time, though, she settled into something like a writing routine. In March 1962 she wrote her long dramatic poem *Three Women* for the BBC (*LH* 456), as well as 'Elm', 'The Rabbit Catcher', 'Event' and 'Crossing the Water' – poems which Diane Middlebrook views as indicative of a subtle change in the hitherto mutually productive relationship between Plath and Hughes. 'Thematically,' Middlebrook argues, 'her poems were increasingly focused on the instability of love, and emotionally they were saturated with dreadful knowledge into which the speaker of the poem is forced to travel.'[26]

By the summer of 1962, the marriage was in difficulties. Aurelia Plath visited for some weeks in July and August but soon sensed the 'anxiety in the air' (*LH* 458). Earlier in the summer, Hughes had begun a relationship with a mutual acquaintance, Assia Wevill. David and Assia Wevill had moved into the Hugheses' vacant London flat after they had left for Devon. The two couples had literary interests and acquaintances in common, and in May 1962 the Wevills travelled to North Tawton to spend a weekend with Plath and Hughes. The relationship between Hughes and Assia seems to have begun at this time and to have continued throughout the summer. In mid-July Plath intercepted a telephone call from a woman she identified as Assia (see the poem 'Words heard, by accident, over the phone') which apparently confirmed her suspicions about Hughes. She decided to seek a separation and to spend the winter in Ireland, resting and writing. In September she travelled with Hughes and the children to Ireland and stayed there with the poet Richard Murphy while seeking a home to which she could return for the rest of the winter; Hughes left his family there and, unbeknownst to Plath, travelled to Spain. From Ireland Plath and the children returned to Devon; Hughes briefly returned to the family home in October, but only to pack his belongings and leave again for London. Plath's letters indicate how traumatised she was by these events: 'The worst things that *could* happen to her *were* happening to her', as Middlebrook puts it.[27] Nevertheless, this period proved unexpectedly fruitful in terms of the creativity and focus of her writing. She told Alvarez that she was working on a 'new novel'.[28] And she began writing the poems which were later to appear in *Ariel* and in *Winter Trees*, explaining to her mother that her routine was to wake early, and then to write 'like mad – have managed a poem a day before breakfast. All book poems. Terrific stuff, as if domesticity had choked me' (*LH* 466). To the poet Ruth Fainlight she wrote, 'I am fascinated by the polarities of muse-poet and mother housewife. When I was happy domestically I felt a gag in my throat.'[29]

By November 1962, the plan for spending the winter in Ireland had fallen through. Missing London culture, burdened by the demands of the large Devon home and isolated from childcare support, Plath decided to return to the city with her young children. She found a flat – in W. B. Yeats's old house, as she delightedly related to her mother (*LH* 477) – and they moved there in December. She was still writing prolifically, reading her work for broadcast by the BBC and meeting with editors (Alvarez of the *Observer*, for example, who had become a supporter and friend). In January 1963 *The Bell Jar* was published under the pseudonym Victoria Lucas (see Chapter 5) and received respectable reviews. By the end of that month, though, a severe bout of flu combined with feelings of isolation (Plath was in a two-month queue to have a telephone installed in her home), childcare shortages and unusually harsh winter weather ('an unspeakable winter, the worst, they said, in a hundred and fifty years' as Alvarez describes it) had affected her badly (*LH* 494–6). Her doctor prescribed antidepressants, and she was making enquiries about finding a therapist. She and the children spent a weekend with friends, returning to London on the Sunday evening. In the early hours of 11 February 1963, Plath committed suicide by gassing herself.[30]

The cause of Plath's death was not widely communicated at the time. American friends presumed that she had died of pneumonia or flu.[31] Alvarez's 1971 memoir *The Savage God* was the first to broadcast the private details of her death to a public audience – a revelation which appalled Hughes (*LTH* 321–6). The *Letters of Ted Hughes* (2007), his 'Introduction' to Plath's 1981 *Collected Poems* and other essays (collected in his 1994 book *Winter Pollen*) reveal something of his motivations and decisions in the immediate and long-term aftermath of Plath's death as he sought both to protect her children and to promote her writing. In the years since Plath's death, her suicide has been interpreted in various ways. For some commentators, it represents an indictment of patriarchy, an inevitable – if extreme – consequence of the pressures on wives, mothers and women writers during this period. For some, the suicide is simply an unavoidable, if terrible, consequence of Plath's history of mental illness. For others, it seems the necessary and therefore justifiable climax of her writing; the trajectory of her career, culminating in the *Ariel* poems, leaving no other route. For others again, and this is a point that Hughes has made in private letters only recently made available (*LTH* 446, 523–4), the suicide is the result of a terrible series of mistakes and coincidences – the separation (Hughes insists that they were discussing reconciliation when she died), the flu, the cold winter, the erroneous prescription of an antidepressant whose brand name Plath did not recognise but to which she had previously had a bad reaction.[32]

The reasons for the death remain as uncertain and as contested as the nature of the life. The portrait sketched above gives some idea of the biographical context for Plath's writing. It sets the scene, but it does not supply all the answers. In any case, it would be a disservice to Plath's ingenuity as a writer to see the work as a mere mirror of the life she led. The intention has been to present the circumstances of Plath's life in as far as these can be known to us as readers (this uncertainty about the status of biographical 'truth' is one to which we will return in Chapter 7), and, while suggesting fruitful connections between some of Plath's poems and biographical events, to indicate the limitations of reading only in this way. In the next chapter we will begin to read the work within broader literary and historical contexts, asking what else in addition to the facts of Plath's life might have shaped her writing, before proceeding in the chapters which follow to look at specific examples of her work in close detail.

Chapter 2

Contexts

The literary and historical contexts for Sylvia Plath's writing are surprisingly broad: she straddles a number of different traditions and discourses. Writing in the 1950s, she is partway through the century and thus might be read alongside the so-called 'middle generation' of American poets. In her early poetry in particular she employs a number of complex forms (*terza rima*, rime royale and so on) to considerable effect, thereby demonstrating her debt to an established poetic tradition. But she also coincides with John Berryman, Allen Ginsberg, Robert Lowell and the early Anne Sexton and thus with the 'breakthrough' of what became known as the 'confessional' mode of poetry. An American by birth, she traces her ancestors back to Germany and Poland and was brought up by parents for whom English was a second language. In terms of literary and linguistic influences, then, she is partway between American and European heritages. Similarly, as an American who moved to England twice, first as a young graduate student then subsequently as an adult woman, a wife and a mother-to-be, Plath embodies transatlantic concerns or, more properly, inhabits, as Tracy Brain proposes, a 'midatlantic position' – one which refuses to choose between two places.[1]

Plath is known as a poet but she saw her real vocation at various times as being a writer of prose fiction or as an artist. She aimed high with her poetry, submitting her work to acclaimed publishers and for prestigious prizes, yet she also had a keen interest in popular culture and a sure sense of the diverse markets for her work. She was a high-achieving writer and mother in a mid-century culture which had few ideas about how to combine these apparently mutually exclusive roles. As Pat Macpherson argues of Buddy Willard's marriage proposal in the 1963 novel *The Bell Jar*:

> In 1961–2, settled in England with her husband, two children and writing career, Sylvia Plath can satirize the absurdity of this suburban kitchen-mat marriage offer. In the early 1950s it was no laughing matter for Sylvia Plath in her journal to try to come to terms with the either/or-ness of motherhood and career, purity and sexuality, domesticity and education.[2]

Writing between the first two waves of modern feminism, her work anticipates many of the issues and ideas that women in subsequent decades were to pursue, but she was deprived of the cultural, political and aesthetic framework in her own time that might have helped her to articulate these. In broader historical terms, Plath's life straddles the uncertain depression years of the 1930s, the anxiety of World War II (an anxiety which as *Letters Home* and *Johnny Panic and the Bible of Dreams* show, she felt particularly acutely as the daughter of a German family), and the chill oppression of the Cold War. Cold War ideology, as Deborah Nelson and Elaine Tyler May, among others, have shown, was itself profoundly ambiguous. At one and the same time, it extolled the virtues of family and home and the security of the domestic sphere, while regarding the private lives and desires of Americans as potentially suspect and thereby worthy of close examination.

Thus we can see that Plath's writing does not necessarily fit securely into any one frame or tradition. Instead, it sits between or moves around several. This mutability may be a virtue. Less positively, the refusal to settle in any one position might be interpreted as a failure to fit in anywhere. Elisabeth Bronfen sees the intensity of Plath's commitments to a succession of different cultural identities as a sign of 'her anxiety that if she did not care excessively about belonging to a given cultural home, she would be forced to acknowledge her deeply ingrained sense of belonging nowhere'.[3]

Literary contexts

The year of Plath's birth, 1932, saw the publication of D. H. Lawrence's *Last Poems*, Aldous Huxley's *Brave New World*, W. H. Auden's *The Orators* and new works by William Faulkner and Ernest Hemingway. By the end of the decade, all the above, alongside Robert Graves, James Joyce, Stevie Smith, Dylan Thomas, William Carlos Williams, Virginia Woolf and W. B. Yeats had published major works. A vital set of literary influences was in place.

Important though the work of these creative writers was, key critics and commentators also exerted an influence on Plath's education, reading and subsequent poetic style. Chief among these was T. S. Eliot, who, in 1932, delivered his prestigious Harvard lectures on 'The Uses of Poetry and the Uses of Criticism'. His influential 1919 essay 'Tradition and the Individual Talent' had already advocated to a generation and beyond the value of 'impersonal poetics' and the importance of a separation between the 'man who suffers' and the 'mind which creates'.[4] The school of 'New Criticism' which dominated American poetry throughout the 1930s and 1940s in part defined itself in relation to the work of Eliot and the other modernists. The New Criticism was represented by the work of Cleanth Brooks and Robert Penn Warren (with Allen Tate, John Crowe Ransom and others). According to Donald Allen, writing in the introduction to his 1960 anthology *The New American Poetry*, a whole generation of Americans (Plath's generation) had been taught to read 'conventional poetry' using Brooks and Warren's 1939 manual *Understanding Poetry* as their primer.[5] The New Critics emphasised the special qualities of literary language. In arriving at an interpretation, they were disinclined to look beyond the poem for evidence either from the poet's lived experience or the reader's emotional response. They were resistant, too, to reading the text within its historical or cultural contexts, preferring to view it as an 'autotelic object'.[6] Their critical practice relied on the technique of 'close reading' or 'making the closest possible examination of what the poem says as a poem' in Brooks's words.[7] A single poem, studied with rigour, focus and sensitivity to the peculiarly literary quality of the language, would yield its meanings to the sufficiently trained reader. It is a critical practice which works best with a particular kind of poem, a poem of complexity, latent energy and tension (Ransom values 'poems [that] are little dramas, exhibiting actions in complete settings').[8] Some of Plath's early work, as Chapter 3 will show, exemplifies such a position and rewards reading in this way.

Eliot and other key figures of the modernist movement, including Ezra Pound, Joyce and Woolf (the last two proving especially influential for Plath's writing), continued to dominate the canon of twentieth-century literature throughout Plath's school and college years and beyond. They were joined by other 'greats': Auden, Lawrence, Marianne Moore, Wallace Stevens, Thomas and Williams. Steven Gould Axelrod provides a list of the authors Plath studied and wrote papers on at high school and Smith College. In her modern poetry course at Smith, for example, 'she read heavily in Auden, Eliot, and Yeats and more lightly in Hart Crane, Joyce, Marianne Moore, Ransom, Stevens, and Thomas'.[9] In her BBC interview with Peter Orr, conducted in 1962, Plath cites her influences as Thomas, Yeats, Auden, William Blake and Shakespeare

(*PS* 170). Tim Kendall's *Sylvia Plath: A Critical Study* notes her debt to Ralph Waldo Emerson.

The influence of Auden's work on Plath's generation of poets cannot be overstated. As early as 29 January 1953, Plath's *Journals* mention reading Auden. The taut, dynamic descriptions in this entry, with its meditations on the 'black bleak angular unangelic nauseous ugliness of the blasted sterile world' (*J* 168), reveal his fingerprint. Plath's contemporary, Adrienne Rich, describes her own similar experience: 'I know that my style was formed first by male poets: by the men I was reading as an undergraduate – Frost, Dylan Thomas, Donne, Auden, MacNeice, Stevens, Yeats. What I chiefly learned from them was craft.'[10] Plath inscribed one of her books of Auden's poems 'I found my God in W. H. Auden.'[11] A letter of 28 April 1953 describes a two-hour reading and seminar with Auden as 'the privilege of my lifetime' (*LH* 110). The poet stood for Plath as one of a succession of colossal idols, mentors or father figures – someone to emulate figuratively and to please literally (Auden was the judge for the Yale Series of Younger Poets prize to which Plath had, in 1957, unsuccessfully submitted an early version of her collection *The Colossus*).[12] By the early 1960s, though, Plath's adulation was beginning to evaporate. *The Bell Jar* offers a veiled satirical sketch of him as the 'famous poet' with the terrible table manners (*BJ* 28). This may have been a consequence of personal disappointment – Plath's defensive rejection of a mentor who was disinclined to accept the role – or it may reflect wider changes in the poetry of the time. The shift from a complex and allusive verse to the freer, looser, more personal forms favoured by Berryman, Ginsberg and the nascent confessional school may simply have prompted Plath to reevaluate her poetic 'Gods'. In her 1962 BBC interview, Plath looks back on her worship of Auden as though it were a thing of the past: 'At one point I was absolutely wild for Auden and everything I wrote was desperately Audenesque' (*PS* 170).

'Poetess of America'

Although, as Axelrod shows (and Rich's recollections confirm), women writers were marginalised on the high school and college curricula, a number of them were important to Plath and her generation. Plath's *Journals* refer, among others, to the work of the ancient Greek poet Sappho, to the Victorian 'greats' Elizabeth Barrett Browning and Christina Rossetti, to Amy Lowell, Edith Sitwell, Sara Teasdale, Edna St Vincent Millay, Phyllis McGinley, Elizabeth Bishop and Moore. In prose, the Brontës, Willa Cather and, most extensively, Woolf merit mentions. Few of the living writers figure as unproblematically positive role models, or as poets with whom Plath might form a bond. Instead, they are viewed as potential competitors. In August 1957, for example, Plath measures her own despair at the latest rejection of the collection of poems that was later to become *The Colossus* by reference to Rich's success, even though, as Plath comments, she considers Rich's poems to be 'dull' (*J* 295). Barely six months later, the resentment is more explicit. After reading the entries for the mere six women poets in the anthology *New Poets of England and America* (1957), Plath declares herself to be 'Jealous . . . green-eyed, spite-seething' (*J* 315).

Plath was writing for publication in a culture which offered fewer opportunities to women writers than to men and implicitly pushed women into competition with each other. The poet Maxine Kumin, Plath's contemporary, recalls of the late 1950s, 'The Women's Movement was still unfounded. An editor of a national magazine wrote me with regret that he could not accept any more poems from me for 6 months or so because he had already published a woman poet the previous month.'[13] Such attitudes persisted beyond the point of publication. Edward Brunner's survey of Cold War poetry shows that poetry by women

> [w]as targeted in the book review process as the central example of how-not-to-write-a-poem. An ongoing but one-sided monologue developed in which book reviews of female poets by male poets sidelined the female poets as effective players. In effect, by perennially addressing the work of female poets in a set of approaches that were repeated from poet to poet, male reviewers virtually evoked a composite portrait of the woman poet.[14]

Lorrie Goldensohn quotes a comment made by Elizabeth Bishop in an interview: 'most of my life I've been lucky with reviews. But at the very end they often say "The best poetry by a woman in this decade, or year, or month." Well, what's that worth? You know? But you get used to it.'[15] In the *Journals* entry quoted earlier, Plath famously declares her intention to be thought of as 'The Poet*ess* of America' (*J* 360; my emphasis), thereby signalling her tacit acceptance of this lesser category of judgement.

Nevertheless, it would be misleading to overlook the value to Plath of a female literary tradition. A number of poets (Emily Dickinson and Marianne Moore among them) emerge again and again in Plath's letters, *Journals* and implicitly in her poems, as models to emulate, rail against or refine. According to Axelrod, Aurelia Plath encouraged her daughter to read Dickinson.[16] Three early poems included in *Letters Home* ('Admonition', 'Parallax' and 'Verbal Calisthenics') demonstrate what Plath describes as a wholly 'intentional' debt to her (*LH* 100–11). Apart from the formal similarities (the use of the hymn stanza, for example), what is the relationship between Plath's work and that of her predecessor? On an obvious level, both poets represent some of the conditions of women's experience in their own particular place and time. More interestingly, perhaps, as Karen Jackson Ford has argued in her important book *Gender and the Poetics of Excess: Moments of Brocade*, both poets devise an aesthetics of excess. A 'poetics of excess' seeks to resist or transgress the oppressive, limiting, silencing constraints of convention. 'Excess' for Ford is 'a rhetorical strategy adopted to overcome the prohibitions imposed by the application of a disabling concept of decorum' or, perhaps, the lessons of the male-dominated, high modernist, New Critical tradition in which Plath was schooled.[17] Although the precise qualities of this 'excess' will vary with historical circumstance, what Dickinson and Plath share is this commitment to testing, critiquing and exceeding the boundaries of a male-dominated tradition.

The relationship with Moore is, perhaps, more ambiguous. Moore was born in 1887 and began writing prose, poetry and a voluminous correspondence at an early age. She was an enthusiastic reader, critic and promoter of the work of the early modernists (H. D., Pound, Eliot and others) and edited the magazine *The Dial* throughout the 1920s. She is a superbly inventive poet; one who takes poetry seriously, is unafraid to tackle challenging forms, and is determined to refine and revise repeatedly until absolutely sure of the rightness of the final text.[18] Moore's importance to twentieth-century literature is manifold. Firstly, she has been regarded as a model by generations of women poets who have seen her sure control of her material as a valuable precedent. Secondly, she has bridged the gap between the work of the early modernists and that of a later generation of more contemplative poets. Thirdly, her innovative use of form and, specifically, her appropriation of 'syllabic verse' (verse which counts the number of syllables rather than stresses in any given line) has provided a distinct and welcome tool for successive generations of writers. Plath tried syllabic verse in several early poems, for example in 'Mussel Hunter at Rock Harbor', which was to be her first piece accepted by the prestigious magazine *The New Yorker* (*J* 347; *LH* 345). As she explained in a letter to her brother, Warren, which urged him to read the poem out loud in order to hear its rhythms, the form was inspired by Moore and gives 'a speaking illusion of freedom' (*LH* 344). Several years later, though, Plath was both mortified and angered by what she interpreted as a rebuff from Moore, to whom she had sent carbon copies of some of her new work (*J* 406).

Confessional poetry

Plath's maturity as a writer coincided with the rise of what has become known as the 'confessional' mode of poetry. Cracks in the façade of the academic verse favoured by the dominant New Critical school were already beginning to appear during this period, hurried along by the work of Berryman, Ginsberg, the Beat generation and emergent poets such as W. D. Snodgrass.

In 1959 Lowell (previously a disciple of Allen Tate) took a new direction with the publication of his collection *Life Studies*. It was in a review of this book that the critic M. L. Rosenthal first identified and defined this new confessional mode. Rosenthal's review characterizes confessional poetry as autobiographical, therapeutic ('soul's therapy' and 'self-therapeutic') and unflinchingly truthful (featuring 'uncompromising honesty'). This direct and personal style was subsequently spoken of as a kind of 'breakthrough' or even 'break out', as though to emphasise its importance in disrupting and escaping earlier orthodoxies.[19] Plath herself spoke of the influence of other confessional poets in these terms:

> I've been very excited by what I feel is the new breakthrough that came with, say, Robert Lowell's *Life Studies*, this intense breakthrough into very serious, very personal, emotional experience which I feel has been partly taboo . . . These peculiar, private and taboo subjects, I feel, have been explored in recent American poetry. I think particularly the poetess Ann Saxton [*sic*], who writes about her experiences as a mother, as a mother who has had a nervous breakdown, is an extremely emotional and feeling young woman and her poems are wonderfully craftsman-like poems and yet they have a kind of emotional and psychological depth which I think is something perhaps quite new, quite exciting.
>
> (*PS* 167–8)

However, her apparent enthusiasm for the mode was tinged with ambivalence. In its own time and since, 'confessional' has been used as a pejorative adjective and applied disproportionately to poetry written by women. It has also been indicted as a popular form which dangerously democratises what had hitherto been an elite field of endeavour.[20] As early as April 1953, commenting on some of the short stories she hoped to place in women's magazines, Plath reveals the low critical esteem in which the confession is held. The 'true Confession' she plans to write (which, ironically enough, is entitled 'I Lied for Love') is aimed squarely at a lucrative market. Having attempted the form, her 'supercilious attitude' towards it has changed. She now acknowledges the demands it makes in terms of plot and tone – skills which are not easily come by (*J* 539). She nuances her position further in the interview cited above, where she attempts to distance the political concerns of her own work from the apparent introspection, even narcissism, of confessionalism: 'Personal experience is very important, but certainly it shouldn't be shut-box and mirror-looking, narcissistic experience. I believe it should be relevant and relevant to the larger things, the bigger things such as Hiroshima and Dachau and so on' (*PS* 169–70). Plath's comments have often been taken as evidence of the difference between her work and that of, say, Sexton. However, it is not clear here whether it is Sexton's example that Plath is attempting publicly to distance herself from or whether it is misreadings of confession as self-preoccupation from which she demurs. For confessional and other poetry of the 1950s and 1960s, as I will now go on to show, has recently been reevaluated as inescapably political, as in fact profoundly concerned with 'the larger things'.

Brunner identifies a complex relationship between mid-century confessional poetry and the traditions that preceded it:

> When confessional verse appeared at the end of the decade it was widely regarded as a break from the academic verse of the 1950s, but if a domestic verse that envisions family members as under siege from the state vies with an academic verse that is intent upon affirming the social unity of the state, then confessional verse may be less a breakaway text than a focusing of concerns that the decade has been struggling to articulate.[21]

The important thing, as Nelson has persuasively argued, is to recognize that confession as a literary mode is not ahistorical or value-free. Rather, it operates in a particular time and place – in postwar, Cold War, suburban America. Nelson identifies a 'double vision' in operation at the end of the 1950s, one we might see reflected in Plath's body of work. This 'double vision' is marked by 'anxieties about intrusions into private life that were largely, but not exclusively, tied to the Cold War; and the uneasiness about the leaking of private life into public discourse that marked the first appearance of "confessional culture"'.[22] It is to the historical and ideological contexts for Plath's writing that we now turn.

Historical and ideological contexts

Plath's historical and ideological contexts comprise a nexus of related fields. These include the legacy of World War II and, with it, a growing public under-standing of the nature and extent of the Nazi Holocaust. This was particularly brought to light in early 1961 with the trial (the first to be televised) of Adolf Eichmann for the enforced transport and murder of six million Jews. Also of note is the emergence of a culture of self-help, self-improvement and popular psychology, manifested in manuals such as Dr Benjamin Spock's 1946 *Baby and Child Care* and studies of the family and masculinity in crisis such as William H. Whyte's *The Organization Man* (1956) and Philip Wylie's *The Generation of*

Vipers (1942) – a vitriolic indictment of overpowerful mothers. Relatedly, the growth of the American suburbs with attendant concerns about adolescence and community and the reemergence of the feminist movement helped to shape the nation's – and individuals' – sense of identity. Parallel with all these was the ongoing struggle for racial equality throughout the century; a struggle which Plath's work comments on only obliquely but nevertheless, as Renée Curry has recently argued, tellingly. In Britain (where Plath lived as a student from 1956 to 1958 and to which she moved permanently with her husband in late 1959), some of the same concerns arise. The impact of World War II was, perhaps, experienced differently in the UK, which had lived through the threat of imminent invasion and persistent attack: in the early 1960s the nuclear threat was felt particularly acutely, in part because of Britain's relative proximity to Soviet bases in Eastern Europe.

World War II

Two stories from Plath's *Johnny Panic and the Bible of Dreams* give an indication of the effect of World War II on a generation of Americans growing up in the 1940s. 'Superman and Paula Brown's New Snowsuit' shows the impact of the coming war on the consciousness of the children. The first person speaker's memories of this time are a kaleidoscopic confusion of winning a prize for a civil defence drawing (*JP* 160) and of the as yet unexplained catastrophe relating to Paula Brown's snowsuit. As the story proceeds, these memories are mingled with others – of listening to *Superman* on the radio (Superman represents an idealised, omnipotent heroism which is played out in the children's games (*JP* 161)) and of myriad childhood cruelties. The familiar references to popular cultural forms sit uneasily – jarringly – with the wider political picture, thereby exposing the duplicity of contemporary American ideologies.

   The story describes the petty bullying of one particular child – a child whose name, Sheldon Fein, implies Jewish ancestry and who is different, effeminate, a 'mamma's boy' (*JP* 161). Sheldon at first tolerates the bullying, but then assimilates and transforms it into his own violent behaviour, including inventive 'tortures' which exceed the parameters of the game. As the story proceeds, the impact of the war becomes more and more explicit. German-American families fear internment and the children's everyday pleasures, such as a birthday trip to the cinema, are corrupted by the horror of the ongoing hostilities. Plath's speaker describes the shock of seeing a short film about the Japanese torture of prisoners. But more shocking still is the way in which this cruelty and brutality are carried over into the children's world. As the story closes, the child speaker who we gather to be of German descent (*JP* 162) becomes the scapegoat, the vulnerable victim of the aggression of her peers. Even the idealised image of Superman fades before the shock of this injustice. As the story concludes, 'That was the year the war began, and the real world, and the difference' (*JP* 166). Plath's mother, Aurelia, records her own experience of such abuse in her introduction to *Letters Home* (*LH* 4). In 'Superman' an adult wartime discourse of violence, punishment, attack, defence and escape is transposed on to the childhood world of the speaker and her neighbours. Those who fall outside the norm in this story, as in the wider world, invite surveillance, punishment or coercion until they, too, conform to the norm.

Another story, 'The Shadow', paints a similar picture. It begins at the outbreak of the war and situates its experience of that conflict in the context of ordinary, civilised domestic life, albeit a life which, as the opening paragraph makes clear, seems subtly to have changed (*JP* 330). Like 'Superman and Paula Brown's New Snowsuit', the story engages with iconic figures of contemporary popular culture – in this case the radio series *The Shadow*. The story is explicit about the vilification of German-American families during World War II and it is complex in its treatment of other ethnic groups, including the Irish-Americans (represented by the Roman Catholic Kelly family) and the Jews. Instead of adult life impinging on the children's world, the children's everyday squabbles are taken up by the adults, causing grown-ups to take sides against the children and each other. Written in 1959 and thus at the height of McCarthyism (see below), 'The Shadow' shows how during this period, certainties about good and evil were subtly dismantled, and a new threat – that of 'the enemy within' – was generated. Partway through the story, the first person narrator begins to realise that she is being ostracised and treated with suspicion (*JP* 336). The story reaches its climax when the young speaker's behaviour in biting another child, Leroy, is excused by a third child on account of the revelation that the biter's father is German. With horror, the speaker realises that in biting Leroy she has unwittingly betrayed her father's origins and exposed both of them as enemies within (*JP* 337). As this blow to justice and fairness and to the American Dream (here represented by the speaker's foolish faith in the FBI, the President and God) sinks in, she sees the civilised world fading into 'darkness' (*JP* 339).

The USA formally entered World War II as a consequence of the December 1941 Japanese attack on Pearl Harbor, Hawaii (the US Navy's main base). Japanese-Americans, like the German-Americans before them, were henceforward identified as potential enemies and a mass programme of internment and deportation was carried out along the West Coast.[23] American involvement in the conflict did not, however, go uncontested. Plath's contemporary and one-time mentor, Robert Lowell, explains his misgivings about the war and refusal to be drafted into the forces in his notorious 'Declaration of Personal Responsibility' of September 1943: 'When Pearl Harbor was attacked, I imagined that my country was in intense peril and come what might, unprecedented sacrifices were necessary for our national survival.'[24] Two years on, Lowell thought that the threat had receded and that the war was being fought on false grounds. He was jailed for a year and a day for his refusal to fight, passing through the infamous West Street Jail (the setting for one of the key poems in his 1959 confessional collection, *Life Studies*) en route to his correctional centre. The war against Germany ended with its surrender in May 1945, but the war against Japan continued. Fear of the number of casualties (American and Japanese) likely to be caused by a conventional ground attack has been cited as just one of the factors which persuaded the USA, in August 1945, to use atomic bombs against the Japanese cities of Hiroshima and Nagasaki. The Japanese surrendered shortly afterwards, heralding the end of the war. As we will see in Chapter 4, the cultural legacy of Hiroshima and Nagasaki informs many of the poems of *Ariel*.

Postwar cultures

As significant as these events are to our sense of the context in which Plath grew up, it is the aftermath of the war which is of major importance to our understanding of her cultural and literary milieu. A key link between the end of the war and the Cold War regime that followed lies in the USA's development and use of the atomic bomb. More relevant still (particularly to Plath's writing) is the Soviet Union's acquisition of the technology necessary to build its own atomic weapons. Plath's *The Bell Jar* opens, as we will see in Chapter 5, with a vignette about the execution of Ethel and Julius Rosenberg, who had been charged with betraying the USA's atomic secrets to the Soviet Union (see also *J* 541–2).

The immediate postwar period in the USA is one of profound contradictions. On the one hand, it is a time of peace and relative plenty (the nation had benefited economically from its role as supplier to its allies during the war). It is a time when women, encouraged by the economic and personal opportunities the war had given them, could glimpse a more independent future, free of the round-the-clock pressures of home. And it is a time when returning black soldiers might have expected some kind of social recompense for the duties they had performed abroad. However, a combination of internal and external factors (residual conflict between the right and left wings in American politics, anxiety about future economic development, the threat from communism in the Soviet

Union, China, Korea and elsewhere) led to a period of anxious, defensive retrenchment. This retreat to the family and the home clearly has particular implications for women, both as poets and in their everyday experience as American citizens.

The communist threat emerges again and again throughout this period. In 1950 communist North Korea waged war on South Korea, which was generally sympathetic to the liberal West. The United Nations became involved, largely under American direction, in order to prevent the fall of South Korea to the communists, and thereby the spread of communist ideas to Western democracies. This fear of infiltration, corruption or invasion by alien forces, underpins American life throughout the period. The USA's involvement in a war against communists in Korea, so soon after the devastating end of World War II, seemed to provide evidence of the deadly and diverse threats posed to American norms. The Soviet Union's development of the technology needed to build the atomic bomb, and its apparent superiority in the space race, added to the USA's sense of vulnerability. In this atmosphere of anxiety, the anticommunist drive known subsequently as McCarthyism could hardly fail to thrive. A deep-seated suspicion about the activities of the communist party in the country led to the organization being banned in many states. The fear was that communists would infiltrate political, cultural and educational establishments, eventually overthrowing the democratically elected government. In 1950 Senator Joseph McCarthy nailed his colours to the mast. The nation, he declared, faced 'a final, all-out battle between Communist atheism and Christianity'.[25]

For the next decade the House Un-American Activities Committee (HUAC) carried out systematic purges of all areas of American life. Everyone was potentially under suspicion; people were urged to be on their guard and to report friends, neighbours and colleagues for anything which might be thought of as 'un-American'. The suspicion and hostility in the *Johnny Panic* stories discussed earlier convey something of the atmosphere. Arthur Miller's 1953 play *The Crucible* famously represents this period under the allegorical guise of Puritan witch hunts. The perceived threat from within was matched, as the Cold War proceeded, by a perceived threat from outside in the shape of potential nuclear attack from communist enemies. This threat came close to home in 1959 with the rise to power of Fidel Castro in Cuba. Cuba became an ally of the Soviet Union, which, by 1962, had begun to install some of its nuclear weapons there. The Cuban missile crisis of October 1962 saw the world apparently on the edge of World War III, though a peaceful compromise was finally negotiated. Plath's *Ariel* poems, many of which were written at this time, evoke the tense climate of the age. This is not to suggest that her poems report directly on these events, but that, as Robin Peel argues, historical circumstances offer a highly charged backdrop for the emergence of 'her own feelings about the madness and destructive tendencies of the men and women around her'.[26]

The decades in which Plath began to write and publish are, then, characterised by uncertainty, menace and an all-embracing culture of surveillance. As Nelson explains, this is both a peculiar, and in the end an inevitable, time for the emergence of the confessional mode of poetry with which Plath's work has been aligned. The 'changing boundaries of public and private domains' heralded by McCarthyism and the Cold War provide fertile ground for the poetry of Lowell, Plath and Sexton. It emerges into a historical and cultural space which simultaneously encourages – even demands – personal revelation while also treating such exposure with suspicion and disdain. Plath's 'Lady Lazarus', who must perform a striptease for which she is condemned, represents what Nelson describes as the 'double-vision' of late 1950s American life.[27]

Domesticity and the suburbs

Concurrent with these ideological changes were other cultural shifts including the changing face of American architecture and family life, particularly in the light of rising birth rates, the return of soldiers from World War II and 'white flight' from the cities.[28] To quote contemporary commentators, 'Between 1950 and 1959, nearly two-thirds of [the USA's] increase appeared in the suburbs; the central cities . . . increased in population by about $1\frac{1}{2}$ during these years; the suburbs increased 44%.'[29] Plath's mother's decision to move to their six-room frame house in the Boston suburb of Wellesley on account of the cheaper rates and good schools is entirely in keeping with the motivations of vast numbers of white American families at this time (*LH* 29).

The new premium on privacy, coupled with economic and technological growth in the postwar years and a desire to reinstate a vision of the natural American order helped to reshape domesticity in this period. As Lori Rotskoff puts it, 'In the aftermath of World War II millions of Americans – at the behest of educators, advertisers, government officials, and producers of popular culture – subscribed to an ascendant domestic ideology that revised traditional familial values for the Cold War era.'[30] It is evident from Plath's fiction, poetry, journals and letters, and from the work of contemporaries such as Sexton, Rich or Erica Jong, that this new domestic ideal was simultaneously an enticing, inescapable and terrible goal. The 'viciousness in the kitchen!' that the October 1962 poem 'Lesbos' spits out represents the speaker's frustration with the ideology of family and home. Of course, it is not only women who felt oppressed by these new ideals. Whyte's *The Organization Man* laments the trap in which modern men are imprisoned. Similarly, as Brunner shows, male poets including Richard Wilbur and W. S. Merwin (with his wife Dido an acquaintance of Plath and Hughes) despair at the lot of the suburban male – bored, trapped, cuckolded.

It is women, though, who as Betty Friedan's *The Feminine Mystique* (1963) reveals, experienced most acutely this intensification of an idealised domestic ideology. *The Feminine Mystique* provides an interesting background to the study of Plath's writing for several reasons. Many of its sources were the kinds of women's magazines that Plath was urgently studying with a view to finding a market for her work. Friedan quotes *Life* magazine's 16 October 1956 view that 'the American woman is winning the battle of the sexes . . . She gracefully concedes the top jobs to men. This wondrous creature also marries younger than ever, bears more babies and looks and acts far more feminine than the "emancipated" girl of the 1920s or even 30s.' More pertinently still, she quotes Adlai Stevenson's commencement address, delivered at Smith College in Plath's graduation year (1955), in which he urged these intelligent, hard-working, presumably ambitious young women to focus those ambitions on husband, children and home. Women's role, he said, was to ' "inspire in her home a vision of the meaning of life and freedom . . . to help her husband find values that will give purpose to his specialized daily chores . . . to teach her children the uniqueness of each individual human being." '[31] As Nelson explains, it was thought that 'cultivating the private space of the home made the greatest possible contribution to the US's success in the sphere of Cold War international politics'.[32]

A corollary of this intense focus on the role of women as instigators of morality in children and men, and as guardians of national virtue, was pressure on women not to betray all this by seeking employment outside the home. In her wide-ranging study of housework and domesticity in twentieth-century America, Ruth Schwartz Cowan explains, 'It is hardly surprising that, in the immediate postwar years, many women struggled mightily with the decision to take a job, since cultural pressures of the most extraordinary kind were being brought to bear against the employment of wives and mothers.'[33] These are pressures which Plath negotiates repeatedly, particularly in her *Journals*, but also in *The Bell Jar*, *Letters Home* and in a number of poems. Perhaps inevitably, these conditions gave rise to a reborn feminist movement. From the mid-1960s, there emerged a new consciousness among some women of the structural and ideological barriers against their full participation in the world. Other countercultural movements emerged at the same time, from the Beats to the black rights movement to a nascent environmentalism.

England

In addition to noting Plath's American origins and experience, it is important to consider the significance of English culture at this time. Plath's initial
excitement on arriving in Cambridge in the mid-1950s lasted, according to
Brain, 'for about a day' and soon gave way to an impression of the nation as
dour, impoverished, and emotionally and materially pinched.[34] Like the USA,
Britain was living through a period of apparent peace and plenty (Harold
Macmillan's 1957 assertion that 'most of our people have never had it so good'
itself echoes the Democrats' slogan during the 1952 presidential campaign).
However, as in the USA, there were undercurrents of disquiet about such issues
as rising Cold War tensions, race and immigration, housing, violence between
youth subcultures and a steadily growing divergence within society between
forces of conservatism and stasis and those of progress and change. In literary terms, these are encapsulated in Al Alvarez's sketch of a tension in the
modern poetry scene between the forces of moderation and conformity (represented by the 'polite, knowledgeable, efficient, polished' verse of the infor-
mal group of 1950s poets dubbed 'The Movement' in Robert Conquest's 1956
anthology *New Lines*) and the voice of radical breakthrough, violence and
change. The latter was represented by the new 'seriousness' and 'depth' and
'openness to experience' of Robert Lowell and Berryman.[35] Plath signals her
approval of Alvarez's view in a comment which also says something about the
hidden complexities of her own work: 'His arguments about the dangers of
gentility in England are very pertinent, very true . . . the wonderful tidiness,
which is so evident everywhere in England is perhaps more dangerous than it
would appear on the surface' (*PS* 23, 32). It is to Plath's early writing that we
now turn.

Chapter 3

Early poetry

Sylvia Plath's *Collected Poems* contains work from all her major collections and is arranged chronologically in order of composition from 1956 to 1963. It also contains an appendix of fifty early poems (Plath's 'Juvenilia') and a list of more than 150 others written before 1956. This is the date which Ted Hughes, the editor of the collection, controversially defines as the starting point of her mature writing (*CP* 15). In collecting and defining this material as 'Juvenilia', Hughes has been accused of marginalising anything that Plath wrote in the years before meeting him, in other words, of dating her maturity as an artist to coincide with his involvement in her life and work. According to Jacqueline Rose, the effect of this is that 'Hughes structures, punctuates, her writing definitively with himself.'[1] While some critics, such as Helen Vendler, agree with Hughes (these early poems, though 'technically accomplished and psychologically truthful' are not yet what she would categorise as mature), others dissent. Linda Wagner-Martin argues that 'Plath was a serious writer right through her college years, beginning in 1950 . . . it seems clear that her poetry should be considered "mature" long before 1956.'[2]

The relationship between the Juvenilia, early uncollected poems and Plath's later works – first the poems of *The Colossus* and *Crossing the Water* but primarily the poems of *Ariel* with which she made her name – has been of persistent concern to Plath critics. For many, *Ariel* represents the pinnacle of her career, the collection for which all other volumes are mere preparation. Peter Davison, for example, writing in 1966, sees anything before *Ariel* as having 'no absolute necessity for being: they read like advanced exercises'.[3] Of late, though, for example in Rose's work, there has been an attempt to recuperate what has otherwise been seen, in Rose's terms, as 'waste'.[4] Tempting though it is to read Plath's work in terms of chronological phases (from the apprentice work of the Juvenilia and *The Colossus* through the 'transitional' poems of *Crossing the Water* (*A Rest.* p. x) to the ultimate achievement of *Ariel*), the drafting and publication history of some of these poems puts paid to such an approach. Some of the early (1956 and 1957) poems are contemporary with those that appear in the 1960 collection *The Colossus*, while others written at the same time as the bulk of the *Colossus* poems were not published until 1971's *Crossing the Water*. Similarly, *Crossing the Water* contains poems which are contemporary with works in *Ariel* ('In Plaster' in the former and 'Tulips' in the latter were written on the same day). Thus we can see that a chronological framework, though helpful to the extent that it identifies broad sweeps of design, tone or subject matter, or shifting personal, cultural, historical or national contexts, does not fully accommodate the complexity of the work. To address this, we need to look at poems in detail in relation both to the collections in which they were first published, and the wider picture of Plath's oeuvre.

Juvenilia and other early poems

The poems represented in the Juvenilia section of Plath's *Collected Poems* are proficient technically (the sestinas, villanelles and sonnets, for example, show a young writer of ambition, handling her material confidently) and include works of psychological and even political conviction (for example, 'Bitter Strawberries' or 'Sonnet: To Time'). However, there are also poems which, in the words of Plath's later 'Stillborn', 'do not live'. They are 'proper in shape and number' but somehow lack the energy or confidence of the poems that follow (*CP* 142). Nevertheless, there is much to interest the reader here. The Juvenilia provide evidence of Plath's long and intense apprenticeship and offer insights into the early seeds of some of her later concerns. For example, the challenge of assembling fragmented and statuesque figures, seen in 'Touch and Go' or 'Gold Mouths Cry' (*CP* 302), emerges later in *The Colossus*, while 'Morning in the Hospital Solarium' clearly anticipates later poems such as 'In Plaster' and 'Tulips' (*CP* 332, 158, 160).

In his introduction to the *Collected Poems*, Hughes remarks on the 'mathematical inevitability' of this early work (*CP* 16). For many readers, there does seem to be a conscious, deliberate, at times rather methodical approach in operation here. Susan Bassnett, for instance, refers to these as 'head poems' rather than ones written from the heart.[5] In 'Love is a Parallax', for example, the complexity of the multisyllabic sounds in the first line alone causes the reader to stumble (*CP* 329–31). So, too, does the emphatic punctuation. The poem has an end-stopped first line, with an apparent caesura in line 2, followed by enjambment, which is brought short by the semi-colon in line 3. The effect is halting. It is as though we are caught in a mathematical conundrum which invites us to proceed but then prevents our so doing. The 'Parallax' of the title refers to the phenomenon whereby a stationary object appears to move when the observer moves their own point of observation – more specifically, it refers to the 'angular amount' (*OED*) of apparent movement. In this poem, then, a mathematical concept is invoked in order to celebrate a richness of other perspectives. These are displayed, in refutation of the exaggeratedly formulaic language of the opening stanza, in images of fluency, fluidity and flights of fancy with 'touches of high rhetoric' as Mary Lynn Broe puts it.[6] The only 'calculus' that matters in the end is the simple equation of 'heart plus heart'.

The complex and demanding rhyme scheme in this and a number of the other early poems is worthy of note. In 'Female Author' the sonnet form (and the conventions associated with it) are used ironically and subversively (*CP* 301). The poem sets up a hyperbolic scene, mocking the female author's implied self-aggrandisement. Thereafter, it descends into bathos, with the author likened to a pet animal, 'curled' on a couch, satiating herself with forbidden foods. Throughout, the poem establishes a clear disjunction between the superficial and attractive surface (the pink and feminine) and the corruption which festers beneath ('sin', 'curses', 'immoral blooms'). Poe-like or Hawthornesque touches reflect Plath's interest in both writers' work. Another sonnet is used in similar manner, to expose the constructed and therefore artificial nature of femininity. 'Sonnet: To Eva' anticipates both the slightly later 'The Colossus' and *Ariel*'s 'Lady Lazarus' (*CP* 305). The poem contemplates the dismantling of a broken or mechanical woman whose grotesque physical breakdown is surpassed only by the final and resounding malfunction of the mind. The final metaphor conjures an image of a bird on a spring coiling out from the open neck of the woman and crying out the time in 'lunatic thirteens'. The closing image reemerges in the villanelle 'Doomsday' (*CP* 316).

The Juvenilia provide several examples of this demanding form ('To Eva Descending the Stair' and 'Lament' in addition to 'Doomsday'). In the villanelle the sixth, twelfth and eighteenth iambic pentameter lines repeat the first, while the ninth, fifteenth and nineteenth repeat the third. One of Plath's examples, 'Lament' offers an early model of the figurative association of father with bees, bee stings and death that we see in the later bee poems of *Ariel* (*CP* 315). The tightness, even claustrophobia, of the form with the inescapable and repeated return to the truths declared in the first and third lines amplifies the trauma of the memory. The poem is riddled with anxieties about chance occurrences which seem, as though in a sort of counterpoint, to rear up threateningly between the moments of certainty asserted by the refrains. This is a tightly compressed poetic form, apparently only just managing the intense emotion of the content.

Everyday life for women in 1950s America is the subject of another villanelle, the often overlooked 'The Dispossessed' (*CP* 318). In this land of plenty, home of the suburban idyll, there is a hidden and horrible underbelly signified by families struggling under the weight of their suburban debt. Again, the poetic form helps to reveal the claustrophobia of the situation. The poem bears comparison with the work of the slightly earlier American poet Phyllis McGinley. McGinley also focuses on life in the American suburbs and often uses the sonnet or the rondeau – a form which, like the villanelle, is circular and repetitious. McGinley is just one of numerous influences in the Juvenilia: 'A Sorcerer Bids Farewell to Seem' – one of the most mannered and self-consciously stylised of these poems – gestures towards Wallace Stevens, while 'The Princess and the Goblins' and '*Danse Macabre*' suggest Christina Rossetti and Theodore Roethke respectively. Other social and political concerns – about the Cold War, the nuclear threat and state violence – figure here. Again, this anticipates the interest of later poems. 'Bitter Strawberries', for example, like 'The Swarm' or 'Getting There', invokes recent European history (specifically, Cold War conflict between the Russians and Americans). Three poems – 'Metamorphoses of the Moon', 'Dialogue *En Route*' and 'Moonsong at Morning' couple conventional poetic images (the moon, the stars and the sun) with a rather more critical and politically charged sense of what such images signify in the atomic age (*CP* 309). 'The Trial of Man' anticipates the opening scene of *The Bell Jar* by juxtaposing the mundane and the violent in its evocation of the 'neon hell' of the electric chair (*CP* 312).

From this small selection of Juvenilia, then, emerge the seeds of Plath's later strengths; the careful, assiduous plotting; the deployment of a range of voices, perspectives and tones; the development of key metaphorical threads; the interweaving of the personal and immediate with larger, political concerns. What these poems lack, perhaps, is the confidence to step free of their influences (of W. H. Auden, Stevens or Roethke, for example) or to range far beyond the framework of conventional poetic form. The more accomplished poems of the later 1950s show her evolution in both these respects.

The poems in the first part of the main body of the *Collected Poems* date, as we have seen, from 1956. Some of these look back to the themes and voices of the Juvenilia. 'Conversation Among the Ruins', for example, shares the same idiom and features similar images as 'Doomsday' and 'Gold Mouths Cry'. However, there are distinct differences. The post-Juvenilia poems use the first person 'I' and 'my' more frequently, and with a confidence and a conviction almost entirely lacking in the earliest work. The 'I' of the Juvenilia talks about what it might or might not do (note the conditional mood in 'April 18'; 'I would not remember you'), speaks in clichés which undermine the authenticity of the utterance (the repeated 'my dear' in 'To Eva Descending the Stair') or is situated in such a fantastic, surreal or invented scene that it cannot be read as anything other than an invention (in 'Bluebeard', for example). From 1956, though, the poems are more willing to assume a personal 'I' and to make the 'I' speak directly from and about immediate circumstances. This is partly, perhaps, evidence of Plath's growing self-assurance as a poet; it may also be, as Chapter 1 suggested, a symptom of the changing poetic climate and a more widespread move towards the confessional. It is evident, additionally, that Plath learnt from the feedback of editors, consciously changing her form and voice in order to secure a chance of publication. Moreover, she encountered a new range of influences and idioms when she left the USA for her Fulbright year in England in 1956.

English influences

The English influence is important to Plath for many reasons. It allows her to immerse herself fully in a literature and culture which she has hitherto studied intensely, albeit from a distance, and it brings her into rich daily contact with a subtly different vocabulary and rhythm of speech. The longer lines and directness of address in some of the poems produced in 1956 arguably reflect this. As Tracy Brain explains, Plath was particularly struck by some of the idiosyncrasies of the English language. Three of the first 1956 poems reproduced in *Collected Poems* use the word 'rook' (the English term for 'raven'): 'It is as if Plath delights in wielding what she thinks of as her newly English vocabulary – a new toy.'[7]

Engagement with the work of English poets such as Hughes was also of obvious significance to the development of Plath's poetics. As Diane Middlebrook notes, Plath's encounter at Cambridge with a group of young, talented, ambitious male poets gave her living models to aspire to. Middlebrook reads across and between Plath's writing and Hughes's, to show the profound poetic effect that their meeting had. Her entries in the *Journals* on and around the day of the *St. Botolph's Review* launch party are full of violent, energetic images which are used of poetry, of the self, of a succession of contemporaries, and finally of Hughes: 'In her morning-after notes, "bang," "blast," "crash," "smash," "wind," and "hunger" become interchangeable terms for lust and for writing.' One word in particular, 'bang', is taken up enthusiastically by Plath and, as Middlebrook suggests, may have been absorbed from Hughes's poem 'The Jaguar' which Plath had read before meeting him.[8]

'The Jaguar' might be seen as a primary influence on Plath's March 1956 poem 'Pursuit', even though, in a letter to her mother of 9 March, Plath identifies a debt to William Blake. In this letter Plath is specific about the shift in her poetic style that she feels herself to be undergoing: 'I have changed in my attitudes' she declares (*LH* 222, 223). Hughes's poem opens with what seems like an Henri Rousseau-like jungle scene (we know from poems such as 'Yadwigha, on a Red Couch, Among Lilies' that Plath was looking to the visual arts for inspiration or confirmation at this time). Yet the vibrancy and exuberance of the wilderness is tempered almost immediately by the bathetic comparisons. Moreover, the jungle of the opening lines proves to be an illusion; this is a sterile, lifeless zoo with fossilised creatures, empty cages and festering animals hidden under straw. The image may have spoken particularly to Plath, whose later work shows an interest in the various forms of pretence which shape and sustain our world, and our complicity in maintaining these illusions.

In 'Pursuit', Plath's figurative response to 'The Jaguar', the Gerard Manley Hopkins-like sprung rhythm, the energetic alliteration and the bouncing and persistent rhyme, which uses frequent half-rhyme and internal rhyme, emphasise the sense that intense emotion is being held under pressure (*CP* 22). The poem opens with a deeply personal perspective on the scene: 'One day I'll have my death of him', the second line declares. This is not to suggest that the 'I' should be identified with the biographical Plath or that the 'him' should be identified with Hughes. Rather, my point is that the speaker/subject is placed here at the heart of the poem, trapped inside with the beast. Hughes's speaker, by contrast, stands outside the scene as one of many observers beyond the bars of the cage. Violent images hammer throughout: 'death', 'hemlock' (a poisonous plant), 'ransacks', 'fury' and so on. The subtle use of different present-tense forms, from the immediate present 'he stalks' of stanza one to the occasional but inescapable use of the present participle ('Advancing always' in stanza one and 'coming always' in the final stanza) emphasises the persistent and inescapable struggle between predator and prey, panther and subject.

Personal and cultural influences coincide in the April 1956 poem 'Ode for Ted' (*CP* 29). Steven Gould Axelrod suggests that this poem, with 'Pursuit', 'Faun', 'Song for a Summer's Day' and 'The Glutton', is written in 'a Hughesian style on Hughesian themes'.[9] The literary antecedents go further back than this, though. The alliterative verse with its mid-line caesurae and its images of greenness, fertility, hedgerows, fields, leaves and woods brings to mind the great Middle English poem *Sir Gawain and the Green Knight.* In Plath's ode 'Ted' is figured as the semi-mythical hero, teasing life out of cold darkness. He is her 'Adam' – a point she makes in a letter of 17 April 1956, four days before drafting this poem (*LH* 233). The emphasis on fecundity and male mastery of the natural world (with concomitant subordination of the female) also brings D. H. Lawrence to mind. Some readers, as Bassnett notes, are 'troubled' by these celebrations of masculine virility – both intellectual and physical.[10] Judith Kroll sees a continuum between the representation of husband or father (itself a troublesome conflation) as Lord of the natural world and the adoration of the fascist which we see in the later poem 'Daddy':

> In unpublished letters she writes of him as a mythical hero or divinity from another age: an Adam who is both violent and creative, a possessor of strength and genius, who would breed supermen.
>   It is obvious that many qualities of this omniperfect husband/god could equally well characterise an omnipotent devil, and in fact part of Plath's presentation of him is as a reformed or reformable destroyer.[11]

The valorisation of the Adam figure in these poems implicitly places the subject/speaker in the role of Eve and inevitably invites the possibility of a fall. Plath indicates as much in the 17 April 1956 letter mentioned above. The preamble to her praise of the Adamic Hughes is a note of caution, indicating that falling in love with this colossus can end only in 'great hurt' (*LH* 233). The natural world and the English tradition are not, then, used unproblematically. Plath handles this new material critically, exploratively and always self-reflexively. 'Firesong', for example, opens with what appears to be an evocation of a richly fertile, natural scene (*CP* 30). Yet it transpires that the natural world is riddled with traps and constantly under surveillance by a spiteful 'warden' (line 4). The speaker's task is to wrest something beautiful, valuable or transcendent (an 'angel-shape') from this oppressively fertile place.

The Colossus

Plath's first collection, *The Colossus*, was published in the UK in October 1960 by William Heinemann and in the USA in 1962 by Knopf. Hughes explains that the collection which finally emerged as *The Colossus* in 1960 had 'evolved' over the years as new poems were included, old ones removed and the title altered at least eight times (*WP* 170–1). Plath had unsuccessfully submitted earlier versions of the collection to seven American publishers (*J* 294). The catalyst that finally made the collection cohere was the seven-part sequence 'Poem for a Birthday' (*CP* 131) which Plath reports 'miraculously' writing in a *Journals* entry of 4 November 1959 (*J* 523).

If 'Poem for a Birthday' was the breakthrough (as we will see later, there are other contenders for this title), it is ironic that it is the sequence that the later American publisher had misgivings about and decided not to publish in full.[12] Middlebrook identifies the origins of this important poem – as indeed of the collection as a whole – in Plath's reading of Roethke's 1958 book *Words for the Wind*, which she encountered at Yaddo in the late summer of 1959.[13] The influence is apparent in the language and tone of both poets' work. Roethke's 'Slug' and Plath's 'Dark House' (part two of 'Poem for a Birthday'), for example, explore the kinship between abject subject/speaker and insect-like object/other. Both use a curious mixture of passive understatement and sheer excitement, which is registered by sporadic exclamations: 'How I loved one like you when I was little!' in Roethke and 'Little humble loves!' in Plath. Both deploy multiple parts or sections in order to explore complex or disparate issues and use images of fruit, flowers, seeds or trees as organic metaphors for an unsettled subjectivity. In Plath's work, as in Roethke's, we are invited to share a sense of the awful chasm which yawns beneath the brittle surface of everyday life.

'Poem for a Birthday' brings all manner of concerns to bear: the search for identity and separation from the mother, institutionalisation, fear, love, despair, violence, powerlessness and transcendence. In the two closing sections, 'Witch Burning' and 'The Stones', the influence is more than solely Roethkean; indeed, some critics wish to demur from the overemphasis on Roethkean models. Marjorie Perloff argues that, 'For Roethke, this world of "lovely diminutives" . . . constitutes a "greenhouse Eden". In such manifestations of plant and animal life, he found the continuity of life and death and understood the organic nature of the universe. It is a vision Plath did not really share.'[14] Other influences, too, hitherto overlooked, are worthy of note. 'Witch Burning', in particular, looks back to a tradition of modern poetry by women (including Anne Sexton's 'Her Kind' and Amy Lowell's 'Witch-Woman') which embraces the figure of the witch-woman as emblem of resistance and transgression.

'The Stones' also has its roots in Plath's own earlier work. The sense of self-loathing replicates the idiom of passages from Plath's *Journals*, while the unforgiving stones and the 'bald nurse' are familiar from 1957's 'The Disquieting Muses' and 1958's 'I Want, I Want'. The synecdochic representation of the self split into body parts is a motif common to the work of other women poets and writers and is recurrent in Plath's writing from this point on. Virginia Woolf comments of her own writing process 'A shock is at once in my case followed by the desire to explain it . . . it is only by putting it into words that I make it whole; this wholeness means that it has lost its power to hurt me;

it gives me, perhaps, because by doing so I take away the pain, a great delight to put the severed parts together.'[15] Wagner-Martin cites Plath's explanation to the American editor of *The Colossus* that 'the collection had a theme, the person who is "broken and mended," beginning with the smashed colossus and ending with the self.'[16] Broe sees 'The Stones' as more than simply an account of the construction of the self; rather, it is a flawed allegory of the construction of self as creator/poet and an account of the attempt to 'restore the speaker to wholeness'.[17]

This tension between creativity and its possible stifling or erosion is a key theme of *The Colossus*, not least in the title poem. Axelrod regards 'The Colossus' as Plath's 'breakthrough' poem.[18] Vendler argues a similar point in a persuasive essay. By carefully tracing the connections between this poem and numerous others, she shows its importance in Plath's oeuvre, defining it as her 'first "perfect" poem'.[19] In a *Journals* entry of 19 October 1959, written while at Yaddo, Plath comments on her work of the previous few days. She notes that instead of her usual 'top-of-the-head matter', she is digging deeper, accessing 'stream-of-consciousness objects'. Out of this have emerged two poems she is satisfied with. The first is 'The Manor Garden' and the other is 'The Colossus', which she describes as being about 'the old father-worship subject' (*CP* 125, 129; *J* 518). The ennui suggested by Plath's dismissive 'old . . . subject' is belied both by her consciousness of the special qualities of this poem and by the intensity and suppressed energy of the poem itself. This may be an old subject, but its treatment is entirely new.

Comments in Plath's *Journals* and in other poems indicate that she arrived at the theme of this poem, drafted in October 1959, as a consequence of revisiting memories of her father Otto. In the previous December, Plath had resumed therapy with Dr Ruth Beuscher and entries in the *Journals* indicate that this gave her the opportunity to assess the effect of the early loss of her father (*J* 429–38). Three months later, in March 1959, she visited the site of her father's grave (*J* 473). In abbreviated and almost defensive syntax ('Felt cheated. My temptation to dig him up'), Plath discloses the personal impact of her return to the site. The word 'stone' or 'stones' recurs three times in this short passage. It is the mute deadness, the 'sallow barren stretch' of the scene, which strikes and depresses her. At the end of the following week, she declares her frustration with the process of revisiting the past (*J* 474), but she also notes that she has just finished the poem 'Electra on Azalea Path' (*CP* 116).

Vendler identifies 'Electra' as one of the key poems which paved the way for the 'breakthrough' of 'The Colossus'. Written in alternating pentameter stanzas of ten then eight lines, the form (and the choice of the classical story of 'Electra' as the frame) enables Plath to blend the descriptive and the contemplative to compelling effect. 'Electra on Azalea Path' resurrects the image of the dead, flat, unyielding stones of the *Journals* entries cited above. It associates the father with the image of bees (a metaphor which reemerges in *Ariel*'s sequence of bee poems and a coded biographical reference to the father's interests). It also implicates the mother in the loss of the father (significantly, in the slightly later poem 'The Colossus' the mother is absent). More dangerously, it implicates the self. In the closing lines of 'Electra', the daughter seeks absolution; the father's abandonment of her is now read as a fault of her own. The specificity of place, the first person narrative of self in mourning and the syntactic form (which Vendler describes as 'an enjambed front-loaded sentence immediately brought up short by a subsequent curt sentence' as in stanza three) all indict Robert Lowell as an influence on the poem.[20] In spite of her early enthusiasm for 'Electra', by the end of May, Plath had rejected it from her forthcoming book as 'too forced and rhetorical' (*CP* 289).

By the middle of October 1959, Plath is back on the theme, albeit this time with a vision which is almost exaggeratedly displaced from the specificity of the scene and relationships in the earlier poem. Although 'The Colossus' opens with the first person speaker (an 'I' that reverberates insistently throughout the poem both explicitly and in the I/y rhymes) it is not at first, if ever, clear to whom this 'I' refers or to whom, exactly, it speaks. Moreover, the opening line establishes an underlying and unsettling bathos whereby the 'Colossus' of the title (suggesting some gigantic and monolithic totem) is undermined by the nursery-rhyme rhythms and allusions. Stanza two conveys the speaker's ennui and frustration at having spent fruitless years trying to clear a way through to the addressee, or to 'dredge the silt' from his throat. Out of this frustration comes daring. She seizes the opportunity at last to speak back to this colossus, to express her anger and contempt: 'Perhaps', she mocks, he sees himself as 'an oracle' or as spokesperson for 'some god or other'. Rather as in Samuel Beckett's 1957 play *Endgame*, the speaker is caught in the position of guardian and caretaker to someone to whom she owes an unknown debt. Her task is ceaseless, thankless and seemingly pointless. She likens herself to an 'ant' and thus her own position is minimised in proportion to the way his is magnified. Stanza four refers for the first time to the colossus as 'father'. The term connotes both a spiritual authority figure (hence 'O father') and a biological one, and the rest of this stanza strives to reconcile the public image, or the 'pithy and historical' figure, with the domestic and private.

As 'The Colossus' closes we see an example of Plath's frequent use of images of the colour red (here 'plum-colour'). At one and the same time, the colour signifies danger, warmth and fertility. The colour red appears in 'Electra on Azalea Path' as well, first to describe the 'artificial red sage' on the grave (sage is the English term for the Latin *salvia*, which, in turn, provides the derivation for the name 'Sylvia') and later and more ominously to describe a different 'redness' that unsettles her (*CP* 117). It is possible to read the closing lines of 'The Colossus' in a number of different ways. For Thomas Dilworth, the poem records the final loss of hope of any heroic rescue by a 'father-figure *ex machina* – Daddy to the rescue'.[21] Both Dilworth and Deryn Rees-Jones proffer persuasive readings of the imagery of 'The Colossus' in the context of Alfred Hitchcock's films, specifically *North by Northwest* (1959) in which the protagonists effect a final, dangerous escape by scaling the vast, sculpted stone faces of American presidents on Mount Rushmore. For Rees-Jones, the comparison with Hitchcock illuminates the extent to which

> "The Colossus" explores Plath's identification and resurrection of the father, at a time when she has returned to her country of birth . . . it points up how the poem is exploring the relationship Plath has between male and female integrated self, her English and American self, playing out both on screen and in still images, part of her continuing mythology of her relationships with men.[22]

The ending also offers an allegory of Plath's self-constitution as a poet, or a kind of manifesto. The merciless conditions of the first section are the necessary grounding for the transcendence realised in the final turn towards the stars and the sunrise. This signifies not surrender but a recognition on the part of the speaker that her subject, and the resources she needs to make something of it, are to hand.

'The Colossus' provides an interesting example with which to consider the question of how to interpret poetry that seems so visibly to gesture towards a biographical context or source. 'Two Views of a Cadaver Room' and 'Point Shirley' also replicate scenes and emotions traced elsewhere in Plath's writing (*CP* 114, 110). In considering these issues, it is important to consider, first, how effective the poems are in transmuting apparently 'real' experience into poetry. What devices and strategies do these texts employ? 'Two Views' employs vivid synaesthesia and a careful, rhetorical stanzaic structure, while 'Point Shirley' (which evokes Plath's childhood experience at her grandparents' coastal home) uses soft sibilance and an elegiac tone in its affectionate binding of self, past and place. Secondly, we need to consider what else these poems do that is not rooted in immediate recall of past personal experience. Both make skilful use of other poets' models. In 'Point Shirley' Robert Lowell's voice is implicitly present, though the idiom and perspective are subtly claimed as Plath's own. The first section of 'Two Views of a Cadaver Room' invokes Plath's experience of visiting a hospital as the guest of her then boyfriend, a medical student – a scene which is played out in turn in *The Bell Jar* (the petulant, self-absorbed and ironically self-exposing voice of Esther Greenwood is anticipated in the voice of this poem). Yet the poem also looks elsewhere. In the second section, Auden and William Carlos Williams are implicitly referenced. Looking to Auden's 'Musée des Beaux Arts' in particular, Plath's poem seeks an insight into the broader resonance of what might, at first, seem merely personal. What is the relationship, the poem asks, between private suffering and public responsibility?

Creativity and self-creation

A number of the poems in *The Colossus* (the title poem among them) are interested in themes of creativity and self-creation. Others are implicitly about the process of constructing and defending an identity. Sometimes, as in 'Hardcastle Crags' or 'Night Shift', this takes place against hostile natural, material or social forces (*CP* 62, 76). In 'Night Shift' the observing subject is in thrall to the mechanistic world around. This poem is presumed to have been written in the USA when Plath returned there to teach after her two years at Cambridge.[23] Nevertheless, to this reader, it retains echoes (literal ones embodied in the clamouring internal rhymes of 'sound', 'ground', 'pounding') of the Northern mill-town landscape of Ted Hughes's native Pennines. 'Night Shift' exposes the struggle to construct and sustain a self (arguably a writing self) in an environment of deafening, machine-like, inanimate forces. These stand literally for the modern capitalist age and metaphorically, perhaps, for the unrelenting pressures of the teaching year Plath was living through. One might even read the factory processes as standing for the kind of technically proficient poetry of Plath's early years – a style from which she was trying to distance herself. The task here is to find a voice, to make a mark in an insensitive, hermetic world. The relentlessness of the night shift which lets the first person 'my' emerge only once in the whole poem is described in the final line as 'indefatigable'. This distinctive word emerges again in 'Words', the closing poem of *Ariel* (*CP* 270).

In some respects, 'Words' recalls the poems of *The Colossus*. The 'echoes' in the later poem mimic those in 'Night Shift', while the 'white skull,/Eaten by weedy greens' brings to mind 'The Colossus' as the figure might look if it had again reverted to a state of neglect. Most importantly, the word 'indefatigable' (the 'indefatigable hoof taps' of the final stanza of 'Words') shows us the other side of the oppression of 'Night Shift'. In the earlier poem the speaker is excluded and silenced. In 'Words' the subject has found a language and a voice and she can declare her subjectivity (hence the emphatic 'I' which ends line 14). For Seamus Heaney, 'Words' demonstrates the ultimate assimilation of poet into language; he sees Plath as 'a poet governed by the auditory imagination to the point where her valediction to life consisted of a divesting of herself into words and echoes'.[24]

Many of the other poems in *The Colossus* register the attempt to find poetic language and thus some form of identity. 'Hardcastle Crags', for example, imagines its speaker striding out through cobbled Pennine streets, striking sparks as she goes. The onomatopoeic 'ck' sounds mimic the sound of her footsteps. The image conjures up a number of creation myths (Prometheus and Frankenstein among them) as well as laying personal claim to the kind of mysterious energy or galvanism which lies behind 'Night Shift'. In 'Hardcastle Crags' the speaker generates her own energy; subsequent women poets, such as Sharon Olds, have seized on the same metaphor to describe their creative impact.[25] This resonant opening is met, though, with a blank, mute disregard. The speaker starts off with such high hopes; like a colossus, she dominates the domestic environment, dwarfing the houses. Yet free of the local and familiar, she can make no sense of what she sees and hears. In stanza five, exposed and alone, she attends to the voices within (or 'babel') and hears only confusion. The biblical Tower of Babel signifies human arrogance and the impossibility of full communication, an impossibility which the speaker concedes when, in the final stanza, she is forced into a retreat. The 'fireworks' with which she proudly set forth are diminished now to form 'mere quartz grit in that stormy light'. In another poem from this collection, 'Spinster', the confused voices of an 'irregular babel' prove to be the subject's potential liberation (*CP* 49). She is given sudden insight – a moment when the chaotic confusion of the world, its 'rank wilderness' as stanza two puts it, is unexpectedly open to her. Yet the rich potential of that world proves too frightening to the 'spinster'/subject who retreats to the world she knows – the familiar and 'austere'.

The refusal of communication (images of 'shut doors' and 'mute' boulders) recurs in Plath's work from the stones of 'Electra on Azalea Path' to the blank incomprehension of 'The Colossus' to the bald, glass, eyeless and egglike faces of 'The Disquieting Muses' and 'I Want, I Want'. These are macabre images, registering the speaker's fear of not obtaining a hearing (it is her audience who are 'indifferent') and, perhaps worse still, her fear of not being able to find a voice, of being silenced, stifled or suffocated. 'The Disquieting Muses' was written in 1957/8 and takes its inspiration and title from Giorgio de Chirico's painting of that name (*CP* 74). As Plath commented in a recording of the poem she made for BBC radio: 'I have in mind the enigmatic figures of this painting – these terrible faceless dressmaker's dummies' (*CP* 276). Kroll points out that this was not the only borrowing from de Chirico; 'On the Decline of Oracles' also refers to his work. Rees-Jones suggests a link between de Chirico's *Enigma of an Autumn Afternoon* and 'The Colossus'.[26] What Plath takes from de Chirico is an impression of a vast, almost surreal, intensely visualised landscape – or more properly dreamscape – 'designed', in Kroll's words, 'to intensify or awaken' emotions.[27] Axelrod argues that the poem 'posits a psychologically momentous struggle with older female figures who threaten to smother or swallow up the female subject'.[28]

Other poems in this collection realise the creative act as an equally painful and even physically damaging one. 'Black Rook in Rainy Weather', though in many ways a celebration of the process of inspiration, also draws attention to its potentially painful impact (*CP* 56). Like 'The Colossus' and 'Hardcastle Crags', it takes images of stars, sparks and fire to connote creativity, illumination or insight. But it also draws attention to the frustrating uncertainty of waiting, in the figurative darkness, for that inspiration to strike. The *abcde* rhyme scheme throughout the poem demonstrates the speaker's poised attentiveness; she has set the scene and, again like Frankenstein, awaits only the spark of life which will galvanise her creation. As though not to frighten her muse away, the speaker declares, 'I do not expect a miracle.' The denial works in Freudian terms as a form of negation, that is, as an example of the way in which 'a repressed image or idea can make its way into consciousness on condition that it is *negated*'.[29] In 'Black Rook' inspiration comes unexpectedly and from the least auspicious of places, in this case from the black feathers of a rook glimpsed in the rain. Its sudden impact is felt physically (it may 'seize my senses, haul/My eyelids up') in a movement which however violent and painful is still preferable to mute, numb, indifferent silence.

In 'The Eye-mote', too, the painful and distorted vision of the artist is to be welcomed in spite of the pain for the new perspective it brings (*CP* 109). 'The Eye-mote' opens with an idealised image of a pastoral scene. The complacency of the vision is realised by the emphatic present participles ('looking', 'streaming', 'striking', 'flowing'); it is as though the apparent perfection will last for ever without progress or change. The vision is disrupted, though, by a painful splinter which embeds itself in the speaker's eye. Vicious though this moment is, compensation comes in the form of an enhanced and fabulous new perspective. What once looked like plain 'horses' now becomes spectacular 'camels or unicorns'.

Throughout Plath's work, poetry is figured as a painful and visceral process. The act of writing is represented synecdochally by metonyms of fingers, arms, mouths, lips and other body parts (see 'The Birthday Present', 'Paralytic', 'Tulips', 'Elm', 'Daddy' and 'Berck-Plage' among numerous others). Her use of metonyms of disfigurement and disembodiment arguably says something about her unease with the role of female poet – particularly in a culture which so carefully polices and judges the norms associated with gender, privacy and public display.

Crossing the Water

Crossing the Water was first published, posthumously, in 1971, though it contains poems which were mostly written between 1960 and 1961 (that is, poems written after *The Colossus* but before *Ariel*). As in *The Colossus* and earlier works, these poems draw on a range of literary models, for example, T. S. Eliot in 'Whitsun' and 'Magi', though the borrowings from familiar mentors (Auden, Roethke, Robert Lowell) are now less frequent. *Crossing the Water* offers a succession of transitions or 'crossings', from one country to another, one persona to another, one generation to another – and even backwards, as in the move from age to infancy in 'Face Lift', and from being to nothingness ('I am Vertical', 'A Life'). These processes of transformation, translocation, even dislocation, though unsettling, are often welcomed as source of a cool, defamiliarising perspective. Images of glass, ice and still water dominate the collection. These motifs help to establish a tension between ceaseless movement or change and moments of frozen, often horrified, inanimation. The impression throughout *Crossing the Water* is of a subject walking on ice, or undertaking a perilous journey and barely managing the 'crossing' without cracking the surface and disappearing into the terrible depths. Many of these poems invoke a sense of great tension, volatility or precarious equilibrium – natural, emotional or physical – which might give way at any moment.

In 'Private Ground', written at Yaddo in 1959 (and thus contemporary with 'The Manor Garden' in *The Colossus*), the gardens or private grounds of the title are poised at the turn between seasons (*CP* 130). The poem's fluency of form, with its occasional long lines (notably the first and last), irregular rhythms and subtle half-rhymes ('peel', 'well', 'all') emphasise the speaker's susceptibility to natural and seasonal change. Unnatural interventions into this scene are captured in the short third lines of stanzas one and three. In stanza one the European statuary, imported from an ancient and alien civilisation, is made to seem out of place, while in stanza three, the 'superhighway' of modern America intrudes. Although the poem opens with the word 'First', it implicitly records the last rites for this landscape as piece by piece it closes (or is closed) down for the winter. The difference between active agency and passive acquiescence is crucial. Other poems – for example, 'Two Campers in Cloud Country' – similarly portray a landscape of extremes, a landscape which refuses equilibrium or proportion (*CP* 144). As the opening line of 'Two

Campers' complains, 'In this country there is neither measure nor balance.' The narrative of stasis and change in *Crossing the Water* necessarily involves the evaluation and reevaluation of the relative merits of passivity and action. Is it better to stay still or to risk change? Another poem, 'Love Letter' (October 1960), opens by attempting to identify 'the change you [an unidentified other] made' but then asserts that the speaker is content to remain as she had previously been; 'unbothered' and 'staying put according to habit' (*CP* 147).

Equilibrium and disequilibrium are similarly explored in 'Event' (*CP* 194). The immediate use of parenthetical dashes and caesurae and the sudden shifts of focus in this poem combine to resist any straightforward synthesis of meaning, while at the same time the first and third person pronouns (from 'we' to 'I' then back to 'we') invite identification and suggest the rudiments of a coherent narrative. The focus changes throughout the poem from a panoramic view of the moon, the cliffs and the animal world represented by the sinister 'owl cry' of stanza two (the allusion is to Act II, scene 2 of Shakespeare's *Macbeth* where the owl's 'scream' is the deadly harbinger of tyranny and, significantly in the context of this poem, presages infanticide) to a close-up shot of the small child, vulnerable in his cot. However, having established this focus – a focus which zooms in from the cosmic to the individual – the poem cannot stop and rest. In stanza four, the vision shifts again, pulling us back vertiginously to show us the cold, hard stars before dropping us again into a freefall which returns us to the intimacy of the moment. The colour palette in this poem, as in so many others in *Crossing the Water* ('Insomniac', for example), is monochrome with flashes of painful blood red and sinister, lifeless blue (the 'cold indigo' of stanza two). Of Plath's own pen-and-ink sketches, appended to the American edition of *The Bell Jar*, the critic Robert Scholes notes, 'These drawings are . . . caught by a meticulous draftsman who understands almost too well what it means to work in a medium where black is the only colour.'[30]

Transformation and change

In addition to geographical change, several poems in *Crossing the Water* deliberate on themes of physical transformation. 'Face Lift' does this in terms of both narrative (the poem, as the title implies, tells of a woman's surgical alteration) and style (*CP* 155). The voice of the poem is mutable and unpredictable. The reported 'I'm alright' in line 3, for example, might syntactically belong either to the other (who is 'whipping off' her scarf and declaring herself to be fine) or to the speaker who is busy reassuring herself that she can cope with the sight she sees before her – particularly in the light of her own self-transforming hospitalisations. Later in the poem, the speaker's narrative is interspersed with, indeed becomes inseparable from, the facelift patient's story. As in 'In Plaster' (discussed below), 'Face Lift' sets up a binary of surface *vs.* depth. Here the depth is not only what remains physically hidden behind the mask of the woman's 'silk scarf' but what lurks in the recesses of the speaker's mind.

The final stanza of the poem, which one might read in the voice of either woman or both, expresses relief at the loss of the ageing and useless self, and pride in the act of self-creation or autogenesis that sees the adult giving birth to the child. The mirror in the final stanza, as we will see shortly in a number of other poems, does rather more than simply reflect the scene. It becomes a kind of repository which, in Axelrod's words, 'confirms the death of an aged, meretricious identity and the birth of a new one'.[31] The disruption of the conventional order such that the speaker becomes 'mother to myself' imbues this whole process with an inalienable sense of uncanny horror. A certain notoriety attaches to 'Face Lift'. As Anne Stevenson's biography of Plath, *Bitter Fame*, reveals, the poem was inspired by the operation that Plath's friend Dido Merwin had undergone.[32] And although, as I have suggested, the poem develops ideas about progression, renewal and change characteristic of this collection, the indeterminate voices of the piece, combined with the mocking detail and the deeply ambivalent ending, make it an indictment of this attempt at self-transformation rather than a celebration of its potential.

'In Plaster' is also worthy of consideration in relation to these debates (*CP* 158). The poem was written in March 1961 (on the same day as *Ariel*'s 'Tulips') while Plath was convalescing from an appendectomy. According to Stevenson, she was simultaneously working on the draft of *The Bell Jar*.[33] Esther Greenwood's voice echoes in the deadpan tone of the poem, its implied bravado and stanza three's rather chilling self-observation: 'I patronized her a little and she lapped it up.' However, the voice is not always as defiant as this suggests. The opening exclamation, 'I shall never get out of this!', conveys the horror of the situation and the isolation of the speaker. Many critics have read 'In Plaster' as an exploration of the theme of the double. There are various different ways of developing this insight. Axelrod argues that the poem charts 'the speaker's growing sense of conflict between alternative identities or body senses – pure and dirty – that vie to possess her'. Elsewhere, he points to this poem's evocation of 'the self's tortured relations with the other' and suggests that the subject is 'suffocated, paralysed, imprisoned'.[34] Persuasive though this reading is, it implies a degree of passivity which the sardonic voice of the poem, and its ambivalent ending, at least partially resist. Taking their cue from this, Alicia Ostriker and Wagner-Martin read 'In Plaster' more affirmatively within a feminist framework. Ostriker calls the poem 'the most brilliant single split-self poem of our time' and associates it with the work of other women writers (and indeed other work by Plath) as an attempt to challenge culturally imposed barriers which prevent women's assumption of a unified selfhood. 'Never far from the surface', she argues, 'is the sense that self-division is culturally pre-scribed, wholeness culturally forbidden, to the woman and the woman poet.' Wagner-Martin, along related lines, argues that it is in this poem and others written in the same period that Plath truly begins to speak as a woman and of 'women's experiences'.[35]

A number of critics have sought to qualify such readings, however. Vendler sounds a note of caution about taking the theme of the double or split self as evidence of schizophrenia: 'Some critics have invoked the word "schizophrenic" in talking about these poems, but Plath's sense of being several people at once never here goes beyond what everyone must at some time feel.' Paula Bennett nuances the 'doubles' argument by implying that this is a relationship of surface *vs.* depth (a theme which, as we have seen, is important in *Crossing the Water*) rather than of competing equals. The emphasis here is less on split selves than on the fissures in the perfect surface which disclose the ugliness beneath: ' "In Plaster," written on March 18, 1961, indicates that Plath knew her façade was cracking.'[36] Although Bennett's point is a valuable one, we may wish to step back from her close identification of the poem's speaker with the poet. The poem works as much, if not more, as a contemplation of larger processes of change and accommodation than as evidence of a specific biographical problem. A final and persuasive way of reading this poem is to consider it as an allegory of the creative process, and specifically of the experience of outgrowing one poetic style and finding another. Broe argues that

> Formally, 'In Plaster' heralds Plath's break with a strict imagistic mode and her discovery of a dissociated speaking voice. The wry irony of 'In Plaster' looks backward to 'The Disquieting Muses' and 'Stones,' and forward to the self-performing spectacles that characterize the *Ariel* poems. In calculatedly naïve tones, the speaking voice has slowly and self-consciously modified its original belief that old yellow and saintly white can coexist.[37]

Her argument brings to mind the comment that Plath made in her 1962 BBC interview, that her earlier work (specifically the poems of *The Colossus*) 'quite privately, bore me' (*PS* 170). Broe sees the poem as a bridge across which Plath had to travel in order to achieve the more flexible and 'vital' voice of the later work.

As the next chapter will show, debates such as this anticipate the arguments about authenticity which have been a hallmark of Plath criticism. Tempting though it is to assess 'In Plaster' in terms of its proper place on the line which is assumed to lead from the Juvenilia successively upwards through *The Colossus* and *Crossing the Water* to the magnificent achievement of *Ariel*, it might be more useful to think about the poem as troubling this trajectory. From this point of view, 'In Plaster' interrogates and thereby complicates the relationship between original and copy, the real thing and mere apprentice work.

Other poems in *Crossing the Water* pursue this idea. In 'Mirror' and 'Crossing the Water' there is a similar identification between, and equivalence of, object and reflection (*CP* 173, 190). Moreover, 'Mirror' works to demonstrate the role of the poetry (metaphorically, the mirror) in producing and not merely reflecting meaning. 'Mirror' is a complex and skilful poem whose potential significance is belied by the exactness of its surface. Constructed in two symmetrical stanzas of nine lines each, it even takes on the physical properties of a mirror. It assumes the mirror's voice as it declares its own attributes, its neutrality ('unmisted by love or dislike') and its ostensible role as mere reflector rather than creator. This self-satisfied hermeticism, though, subtly gives way to something rather more creative and productive. Although on one level the mirror continues simply to replicate what it sees before it, on another – and specifically in the poem's lengthening closing lines – it assumes an altogether more creative, imaginative role. It is as though the reflection exceeds the edges of the frame. Rather like the eponymous painting in Oscar Wilde's *The Picture of Dorian Gray* (1891), it assumes an uncanny life of its own.

For M. H. Abrams, writing in the highly influential *The Mirror and the Lamp*, art can be either mimetic or expressive; its role is either to reflect what lies before it or to express what lies beneath. Arguably, Plath's poetry works in both ways. In 'Face Lift', 'In Plaster' or 'Mirror,' it reflects a scene (either real or imagined) and it expresses complex ideas and emotions – perhaps by processes of displacement and condensation similar to those which Freud identifies in dream work. But what these poems are also beginning to do – and this becomes more evident still in *Ariel* and later poems – is to use language as a way of creating reality, meaning and subjectivity. For Perloff, a characteristic of subsequent, avant-garde and postmodernist poetry is a turn away from '*authenticity*' and 'toward *artifice*, toward poetry as making or praxis rather than poetry as impassioned speech, as self-expression'.[38] This offers a suggestive way of reading some of Plath's work. Chapter 7 will show that recent Plath scholarship (and theoretical work on confession more generally) has been interested in the ways in which language constructs subjectivity and truth. Stimulated by Plath's use of the motif of the mirror, it might be rewarding to think about the ways in which her work escapes or exceeds the limitations of the biographical (as, for example, the reflection broaches the frame of the mirror in the poem of that name) and creates new subjectivities, new landscapes (physical and psychic) and new experiences.

Many of the poems of *The Colossus* ('The Manor Garden' and 'Metaphors', for example) link fertility in the natural and human spheres with aesthetic creativity. A loosely related group of poems in *Crossing the Water* (notably 'Magi' and 'Small Hours' – also known as 'Barren Woman') reinterrogate this connection or ask about the dreadful consequences of the funnelling away or depletion of creativity hinted at elsewhere (*CP* 148, 157). In 'Magi', as in *The Colossus*'s 'The Disquieting Muses', a girl child is accompanied by ambivalent mentors or guides. The title of the poem looks back to male literary models (Eliot and Auden) in its attempt to find sure ground in which to root the daughter's development. Beyond this, of course, the title looks back to the biblical story of the birth of Christ – as appropriate a setting as any, it would seem, to celebrate the arrival of the infant in the poem. Yet the model proves ambiguous; throughout, the poem grapples with a selection of indeterminacies (the 'abstracts' which 'hover like dull angels'), while the 'Magi' themselves present the exact same inscrutable, blank, egglike faces seen in numerous other poems. These frightening emblems of silence offer a perpetual symbol of frustrated creativity and a dreadful warning of what might come to pass for the girl child.

Perhaps the best known of Plath's poems in this vein is 'Stillborn' (*CP* 142). 'Stillborn' is also about the intractability of language, its refusal to say just what is meant (to paraphrase Eliot's 'The Love Song of J. Alfred Prufrock'). The interesting aspect of the much-quoted opening line of this poem (which declares that these lines 'do not live') is that it nuances the concept of living, or blurs the boundaries between life and death. As the text goes on to show, it is not that the poems are dead, exactly, it is that they lack life. The distinction is important. The poems, we are told, have all their faculties; their limbs are in the right places, but somehow they are missing that spark or vital force that other poems ('Black Rook' or 'Hardcastle Crags' in the earlier collection) had managed to grasp. As the final stanza shows, from the lifelessness of the offspring it is but a small step to the lifelessness of the speaker/mother/poet. This is an inversion of the trope found elsewhere in Plath's and indeed other poets' work (for example, in Anne Bradstreet's c.1666 'The Author to her Book') whereby biological and artistic creativity are entwined. In 'Stillborn', as in other poems ('Last Words', 'Widow', 'Parliament Hill Fields'), poetry – instead of symbolising female potential and fulfilment – stands for stiflement and a solemn silencing. The falling rhythms and long melancholy lines, particularly of the final stanza, exemplify the loss of hope and corresponding abandonment of form.

Displacement

There is a recurring concern in this collection about dislocation; speakers frequently feel themselves to be out of place or out of time. 'Blackberrying' and 'Wuthering Heights' both exemplify this concern (*CP* 168, 167). 'Blackberrying' (written in England in September 1961) seems truly sickened by the scene it invokes. The apparently harmless rural pastime of picking blackberries from the late summer hedgerows becomes emblematic of the speaker's sense of isolation and despair. The mood is intensified by the nightmarish setting in which all colours (the 'high, green' of the fields and the 'orange rocks' of the hills), all sounds and all tastes seem exaggerated, garish and obscene. The emphatic opening line, beginning with the word 'nobody', and the repetition of the refrain 'nothing, nothing' that brings the first and last stanzas together, highlight the speaker's solitariness. She is squeezed and thus suffocated between the blackberry walls of the lane (metaphors of funnels and alleys emerge repeatedly in these poems and figure the threat of personal diminishment), then threatened with expulsion into a dead sea. The blackberry walls throw out hooks to catch at her, each seemingly final hook (for example, at the end of stanza two) succeeded by yet another (the 'last hook' of stanza three) as though to emphasise the persistent threat posed by this claustrophobic scene. Release, when it comes, delivers 'nothing, nothing' but a punishing seascape with the tide 'beating' on the shore.

In 'Wuthering Heights' it is not only the subject who seems disconnected from her environment, it is the environment itself which is subject to change, or 'unstable' as line 2 puts it. In an entry in the *Journals* of around December 1958 (included as an appendix to *The Journals of Sylvia Plath*), Plath describes her actual visit to the setting of Emily Brontë's 1847 *Wuthering Heights* (*J* 589). A slightly earlier entry included in the main body of the *Journals* sketches out some ideas based on the visit to the moors and indicates an early plan to create a narrative using four voices (*J* 303). Joyce Carol Oates argues that in 'Wuthering Heights' 'Plath is an identity reduced to desperate statements about her dilemma as a passive witness to a turbulent natural world.'[39] However, we might argue that the speaker is more involved than this suggests – that identity and place are shown to be mutually constitutive. Rose makes a similar point with respect to Plath's 'poems about encounters with the natural world'. These, she says, 'establish the speaker's interaction with that world, not as passive, but along lines better understood in terms of a reciprocating activity or even desire'.[40]

Nevertheless, the speaker clearly feels herself to be threatened in this place. The wind, which in stanza two is likened to her 'destiny', tries to siphon her life away. Similar motifs of draining or depletion figure in 'Private Ground' and other *Colossus* poems and in *Crossing the Water*'s 'Insomniac', where the subject's night-time thoughts drain away 'like water out the hole' (*CP* 163). So, too, in 'Parliament Hill Fields' the voices of the schoolchildren the grieving speaker encounters on her walk are 'funnelled off', in an indication of her isolation and vulnerability (*CP* 152). In 'In Plaster' this fear of leakage or depletion becomes the final threat made by the shrivelled yellow body inside the plaster cast: 'she'll perish with emptiness then' (*CP* 158). 'Last Words' is even more explicit about the implications of such losses; the poem describes the evacuation of the 'spirit' or life-force which 'escapes like steam' through 'mouth-hole or eye-hole' (*CP* 172). 'Last Words' closes with the speaker's resolution to be whole unto herself, to look within for the precious resources she requires. Rather as at the end of 'The Colossus', this implies either surrender to an inevitable fate – abandonment, isolation, neglect – or a positive affirmation of the value, in poetic terms, of the speaker's own resources.

Chapter 4

Ariel and later poetry

In November 2004 Frieda Hughes issued a new edition of Sylvia Plath's best-known collection. *Ariel: The Restored Edition* (subtitled 'A Facsimile of Plath's Manuscript, Reinstating Her Original Selection and Arrangement') embodies, while attempting to lay to rest, debates about the status of this work. *Ariel: The Restored Edition* presents for the first time the sequence of poems in the order Plath herself seems to have intended. The volume includes a foreword by Frieda, a facsimile of Plath's complete typescript and a copy of working drafts of the title poem. I will refer to this edition as relevant in the discussion below and in particular when considering the late poems which, according to the first typescript of *Ariel* (now held at Smith College library) were part of Plath's original arrangement, though omitted from the first edition. However, the bulk of my argument will be based on my reading of the first published version. This is the *Ariel* that, for forty years, has been circulated, studied and discussed and the version which Plath criticism has, until now, taken as its focus.

The poems of the first edition of *Ariel* were mostly written, as Ted Hughes indicates in his introduction to the *Collected Poems*, between July and Christmas of 1962. In a letter of 16 October 1962, Plath calls them the best poems of her life; poems which 'will make my name' (*LH* 468). *Ariel* was initially published in London by Hughes's publisher, Faber and Faber, in 1965 and in New York the following year by Harper & Row. These slightly different UK and US versions comprise the selection and arrangement of poems undertaken by Hughes in approximate accordance with the order of the poems that Plath left in a black ring-binder at her death; the extent of his editorial involvement was barely scrutinised at the time. Subsequently, Hughes was quite clear about his role in choosing and ordering poems for the volume. In a 1971 piece for the *Observer* newspaper (reprinted in *Winter Pollen* as 'Publishing Sylvia Plath'), Hughes outlines the original shape of the collection, and some of the circumstances which persuaded him to publish it in the form the 1965 edition took (*WP* 163–9). In a note to the 1981 *Collected Poems*, he lists the selection and arrangement of *Ariel* as Plath had left it (*CP* 295) and in his 1995 *Paris Review* interview, 'The Art of Poetry LXXI', he further clarifies his editorial rationale. He explains that he chose most of the poems that Plath seems to have planned to publish in *Ariel*, adding a few others that she had begun to write after she considered the *Ariel* manuscript closed and removing those he considered, at the time, too painful and uncomfortable for surviving family and friends (and presumably, as subsequent critics have complained, for himself). Hughes points out that 'within six years' of the publication of *Ariel*, all the poems in the group – including the contested ones – had been published in some form. In defence of his strategy, he raises a pertinent question about Plath's working habits, a question which looks back to the long-winded gestation of *The Colossus*: 'How final was her order?' he wonders; 'she was forever shuffling the poems in her typescripts – looking for different connections, better sequences. She knew there were always new possibilities, all fluid.' Hughes's involvement in the posthumous design of this volume has, nevertheless, given some commentators cause for concern. As he concedes, 'I have been mightily accused of disordering her intentions and even suppressing part of her work.'[1] Chief among the critics of his actions is Marjorie Perloff whose 1984 essay 'The Two *Ariels*: The (Re)making of the Sylvia Plath Canon' asked timely questions about the difference Hughes's editorial decisions had made to the shape and reception of the book.[2] The point has been taken up and developed since by critics such as Susan Van Dyne and Lynda K. Bundtzen.

Equally important is that contentious and persistent debates have arisen around the question of the relationship between these late poems – the poems which made Plath's name – and her earlier work. For some, as noted previously, the early poems of *The Colossus* and *Crossing the Water* are only significant as groundwork for the subsequent achievement of *Ariel*. In the discussion which follows, I will implicitly evaluate the merits of such a reading, in part by assessing the qualities of the poems themselves, and in part by indicating their debt to or resolution of, the thematic and formal concerns of the earlier work. How well does *Ariel* work as poetry, and what does it do differently or better than the previous poems?

Ariel

In *Ariel* Plath's earlier interest in doubles is transformed into a preoccupation with the uncanny ('Death & Co.'), with unsettling child doubles ('Morning Song') and with strange things in unfamiliar places ('Poppies in October'). The sound of the echo dominates the collection (in 'Morning Song', 'Elm', 'Nick and the Candlestick' and the final poem, 'Words', for example) and is accompanied by the related motif of the bell which is also a death knell ('Death & Co.', 'Sheep in Fog', 'Berck-Plage', 'The Moon and the Yew Tree'). Together, these suggest reverberating sound which bounces from surface to surface and then carries across borders and into the unknown. Christina Britzolakis points out that these poems, more than the earlier work, rely on 'oral/aural, incantatory element[s] at the level of language' and Plath herself specifically comments on the thrill of reading these poems out loud (*PS* 170).[3] Images of thwarted escape or entrapment evident in earlier work reemerge here in the 'hooks and cries' of 'Berck-Plage', 'Elm', 'Tulips' and 'Ariel'. The horror of imminent suffocation by smoke ('Fever 103°', 'The Bee Meeting') or fog ('Sheep in Fog') or veils ('Fever 103°', the bee sequence) is startlingly realised in the panicky cry of 'The Moon and the Yew Tree': 'I simply cannot see where there is to get to' (*CP* 172). This is both a literal conundrum (she cannot see the way), a figurative one (she is not sure where to turn for help) and an aesthetic one – some sort of creative dead end has been reached. In order to break through this crisis of expression, the poems must devise and exercise ever more ingenious, elliptical or forceful strategies. Images of blankness and stasis (what Britzolakis reads as 'images of entombed voice') such as those we have seen in earlier collections are here synthesised into an even more pervasive sense of dumb inarticulacy – 'the voice of nothing' as 'Elm' puts it, the 'shrunk voices' of 'Berck-Plage', the 'blackness and silence' of 'The Moon and the Yew Tree' and the failed or missing fingers and tongue of 'Paralytic'.[4] Again and again in *Ariel* we witness the subject in fragmentation or dissolution: 'I break up in pieces' ('Elm'), 'I unpeel' ('Ariel'), 'your gestures flake off' ('The Night Dances'), 'my selves dissolving' ('Fever 103°'). This is experienced in contradictory ways as a loss of agency (in the final poem, 'Words', 'fixed stars govern a life') and as the necessary precursor to some form of rebirth ('Getting There', 'Fever 103°', 'Stings', 'Ariel', 'Lady Lazarus').

Echoes

The motif of the echo appears first and explicitly in the opening poem, 'Morning Song', where the cry of the newborn baby echoes back and forth between infant, parents and midwife ('our voices echo') (*CP* 156). The syntax of the line confirms the separateness of infant from parents and, paradoxically, their communality (in order to make a sound, both parties must reciprocate each other's cry; the allusion is to the nymph Echo in Ovid's *Metamorphoses*). Diane Middlebrook cites this poem as a key example of the complex and equal relationship between Plath and Hughes. His poem 'Lines to a Newborn Baby' is echoed in her 'Morning Song' and then echoed back again in his 'Full Moon and Little Frieda'.[5] In addition to this thematic use of the echo, the device is used covertly in a number of poems in the repeated use of exact words or phrases: 'echoing, echoing' in 'Elm' or 'talk, talk, talk' and 'marry it, marry it, marry it' in 'The Applicant'. One effect of this trope is to suggest that the subject is somehow trapped in language, that the words echoing around her form an unbreakable barrier – almost like a bell jar – which offers no way out. Images of mirrors and other reflective surfaces (in 'The Couriers' or 'Berck-Plage', for example) offer a visual representation of this effect. We will return to this wider use of doubling or repetition shortly.

As indicated above, in classical mythology Echo is the wood nymph in Ovid's story of Narcissus. Echo is unable to speak until spoken to; more chillingly, she 'cannot stay silent when another person speaks; but yet has not learned to speak first herself'.[6] Rejected by the beautiful youth Narcissus, she fades away into the woods and caves until only her voice remains. The myth gives us the seeds of a tension which figures throughout *Ariel* between silence and voice. Echo's plight – having to speak against her will and being unable to speak when she wishes – offers a key to contradictory moments in the book. The 'shrunk voices' of 'Berck-Plage' and the 'voicelessness' of 'The Munich Mannequins' contrast with the defiant 'shriek' of 'Lady Lazarus' or the declarative, even performative 'I'm through' of 'Daddy'. The classical myth also helps us to read the movement towards dissolution in *Ariel*, or the gradual erosion of self until little more than voice remains. For example, the closing 'nowhere' of 'The Night Dances' references both the disappearance of place and the attenuation of self, which no longer seems to exist anywhere (*CP* 249). The 'selves dissolving' in 'Fever 103°' continue the theme, while in 'The Moon and the Yew Tree', more terribly still, not even voice remains. There is only 'blackness and silence' (*CP* 231, 172).

This and other mythological stories of desire, loss, pain and revenge provide a framework for the rest of the collection. In 'Little Fugue', for example, the speaker revisits the death of the father, while in 'Nick and the Candlestick' the love of the child is inextricable from a sense of the precariousness of his existence and the apparent imminence of his loss (*CP* 187, 240). This apostrophe to the son is notable for its sinister and threatening images: the 'Bat black airs' and 'cold homicides', the 'vice of knives' and the 'piranha'. Even the image of the miner's lamp in stanza one encodes a threat; coalminers' lamps burnt oil or paraffin, but the flame showed blue in the presence of a potentially lethal mix of methane gas and air. In an underground cave of suffocating 'blue' (the colour is used elsewhere by Plath, for example in 'Parliament Hill Fields', to signify asphyxiation), the speaker attempts to construct a soft, warm, red, womblike space. Her profound love for the baby (the 'love, love' in stanza ten) and the exaggerated comparison with the baby Jesus in the last line seem constantly threatened by the possibility of his loss. Allusions to invisible poison (the methane gas implicitly turning the flame blue in stanza one, the 'mercuric/Atoms' of the penultimate stanza) show that the threat is not merely personal. 'Nick and the Candlestick', with other Plath poems written at this time, registers a fear, felt particularly acutely in this period, of impending atomic catastrophe – it was drafted, Robin Peel points out, at the height of the Cuban Missile Crisis of 22 to 29 October 1962. With this background in mind, we can better understand the pervasiveness of the images of death, destruction and despair in the poem, and the desperate hope that this child might not only survive but also, somehow, be the salvation of others.[7]

A slightly earlier poem, 'Elm' (March 1962), shares some of the same pervasive anxieties (*CP* 192). In some ways an atypical poem, 'Elm' adopts the voice of the eponymous tree. This ventriloquism (seen more obviously in *Crossing the Water* poems such as 'Zoo Keeper's Wife' and 'The Surgeon at 2 a.m.') caused some confusion on the poem's completion. According to Bundtzen, Howard Moss, poetry editor of *The New Yorker* at the time (Plath had a contract with *The New Yorker* which gave it first refusal on all her poems) was 'worried about whether readers [would] understand that the voice in the poem belongs to Elm and insist[ed] the title be changed to "Elm Speaks"'. Bundtzen notes that Plath was – as usual – ' "delighted" ' to have the poem accepted at all and thus willing to accede to the change of title. For Middlebrook, the poem registers 'a shift in the emotional dynamics between herself and her husband'.[8] However, we might also say that 'Elm', like 'Nick and the Candlestick', ranges more widely than this and uses phenomena from the natural world in order to register not only personal unease, but also a sense of larger crisis or breakdown in the social world. For Louis Simpson, 'Elm' is a poem which speaks not only (if at all) of personal trauma, but first shoulders and then voices collective fears.[9]

This displacement of the human on to the natural is often a feature of Plath's work, offering a way of achieving both distance from, and some kind of grand or mythical context for, what might otherwise seem too close and immediate. The Roethke-inspired poems of *The Colossus* and *Crossing the Water* do this to a certain extent. What is different in 'Elm' is that Plath does not just displace and describe these connections between disordered self, society and natural world, she embodies them by assuming the voice of the tree. Anne Sexton's 'Where I Live in this Honorable House of the Laurel Tree', published in her 1960 collection *To Bedlam and Part Way Back* and thus known to Plath, adopts a similar strategy, this time appropriating the voice of the mythical character Daphne (again from Ovid's *Metamorphoses*). Daphne, who is fleeing her suitor, appeals to her father Peneus to save her from his approaches. He complies by turning her into a tree: 'her soft breast was enclosed in thin bark, her hair grew into leaves, her arms into branches, and her feet that were lately so swift were held fast by sluggish roots'.[10] Chillingly, her escape becomes a new form of imprisonment. We can speculate about how this myth might have appealed to Plath and see echoes of the Daphne story in the opening lines of 'Elm' alone with its reference to fear-induced despair and the 'great tap root' which grounds this knowledge. As Hughes shows, 'Elm' is among the earliest of the *Ariel* poems and one of its most significant. During the drafting process, something changed:

> The lines try to take the law into their own hands. She forced the poem back into order, and even got a stranglehold on it, and seemed to have won, when suddenly it burst all her restraints and she let it go.
> And at once the *Ariel* voice emerged in full, out of the tree. From that day on it never really faltered again.   (*WP* 187–8)

What is it about 'Elm' that is so striking and, for Hughes at least, so emblematic of the 'voice' of *Ariel*? From the outset, the poem is explicit in its acknowledgement of, and more importantly its struggle with, trauma and despair. Where in other poems the speaker's sense of fragmentation and dissolution are projected on to external objects (the disturbed mirror of 'The Couriers', for example), here they are internalised by the tree/self which breaks up in pieces. Similarly, where earlier poems are unable to settle or rest, here the kinetic energy is concentrated in one place. The tree seems charged, throwing off sparks of concentrated energy – hence the scorched 'red filaments' of stanza six. Flat and restrictive seascapes; unyielding, merciless moons; punishing regimes of hospital treatment which leave the speaker 'diminished and flat'; loved ones who hook and trap the speaker, turning her from ally into prey: all these emblems, each of which is repeated throughout Plath's oeuvre, coalesce here. In this tree the speaker's worst fears conspire to the extent that she can take no more: 'I am incapable of more knowledge', as the penultimate stanza has it. Having said this, confessional poetry (a label that has often been applied to *Ariel*) is typically spoken of as a mode which takes risks, which is characterised by the bravery of the speaker in facing up to his or her own demons. We might argue that in 'Elm' we see the subject daring to look her worst fears in the eye. The metaphor of the tree and the assumption of its voice offer her the strength and stillness to take on this task. A similar quest for a firm and dependable base is found in 'Nick and the Candlestick', which identifies in the baby an enviable self-assurance and strength; he is the sole 'solid the spaces lean on'.

Other poems enact various practices of self-sacrifice or martyrdom or engage in some form of libation. The title poem 'Ariel' imbibes 'sweet blood mouth-fuls' on its passage from 'darkness' into the fierce 'red/Eye' of the morning (*CP* 239). The 'cauldron' of morning might signify some kind of crucible of life and thus rebirth or, alternatively, a melting down and thus dissolution of self. The implied homophone of 'morning'/mourning also embodies these contradictory interpretations. 'Berck-Plage', too, closes with a motif of sacrifice (*CP* 196). This austere elegy opens with macabre and surreal images and offers a chillingly flat exposition of melancholia. The two-line stanzas throughout each of the poem's seven parts emphasise the speaker's dissociation from the scene and the apparent disconnection of her thoughts as they stagger from observation to question to assertion. The disconnection, though, is less certain than the stanzaic structure suggests. Disparate parts of the poem are connected by specific threads, while the aural properties of the language form one par-ticular strand which ties together the whole, long lament. The onomatopoeic 'hiss of distress' at the end of part one prepares us for the 'shrieks' and 'sighs' of part two and the 'cries' of part three, which in turn take us to the dead man's now silent 'tongue' in part five and the 'naked mouth' of the grave in the final section.

'Berck-Plage' opens with the same disappointment in the natural world that we have seen in other poems. The sea, though archetypically the source of life and a symbol of fertility (its cyclical tides, like the rhythms of the female body, are associated with the power of the moon), fails to deliver its promise: 'this is the sea, then', the poem opens laconically, 'this great abeyance'. The colours here, as in 'Eye Mote' and 'Blackberrying', are seen in high relief. The startling greens and reds seem to represent a kind of hyperreality, a vividness of detail which throws the speaker's own blank, steely, colourless vision into sharp perspective. Hughes indicates in the notes to this poem that the 'Berck-Plage' of the title refers to 'a beach on the coast of Normandy, which SP visited in June 1961. Overlooking the sea there was a large hospital for mutilated war veterans and accident victims.' The funeral, he explains, is that of a Devon neighbour who died the year after the Normandy visit (*CP* 293). The sketch 'Rose and Percy B' (*JP* 226–39) offers a prose narrative of the actual events mediated in the poem. 'Berck-Plage' supplies little by way of reassurance (to that extent it deviates from the elegiac tradition, which typically closes with some kind of promise or succour). The man's death is dehumanised, rendered impersonal: 'there is no hope, it is given up', as the final line declares flatly. 'It is given up' suggests that the death is a form of sacrifice or offering, made for some higher purpose which the poem itself is unable to articulate.

The bee sequence, 'Lady Lazarus' and 'Daddy'

The bee poems, too, though often read as a 'parable of female self-assertion, or as a narrative rite of rebirth' might alternatively be seen as an account of 'scapegoating' and sacrifice.[11] The bee sequence includes 'The Swarm' (in the US edition of *Ariel* only), 'The Bee Meeting', 'The Arrival of the Bee Box', 'Stings' and 'Wintering' (*CP* 211, 212, 214, 215, 217). The last four, in this order, were as Plath planned to close the volume. Hughes changed this, substituting 'Kindness', 'Contusion', 'Edge' and 'Words' in their place. Perloff and Bundtzen have critiqued this decision, pointing out that in Plath's arrangement *Ariel* begins with the word 'Love' and ends with the word 'spring'. Moreover, the larger trajectory of the bee sequence, leading from isolation to community, innocence to experience, stasis and death to new life and hope, potentially casts the whole of *Ariel* in an entirely different light.

In 'The Bee Meeting' the speaker is unsettled by the unfamiliar scene. The rhetorical questions which recur throughout signal her unease and confusion. She senses a conspiracy and thus feels vulnerable (as at the beginning of stanza two) and powerless (at the end of stanza three, she is passively 'led'). The arcane rituals of the bee meeting are all the more alarming for being surreally juxtaposed with the everyday and domestic – 'strips of tinfoil' and 'dusters'. The initiation the frightened woman undergoes is tacitly likened to a wedding scene; she wears a veil and is attended by a vicar and a midwife who are witnesses to her defloration. 'The Arrival of the Bee Box' traces the implications of the speaker's initiation into this group. The opening phrase, 'I ordered this', has the same force as the admission 'I've done it again' in 'Lady Lazarus'. In both cases, the statement works as an assertion of power and as a rueful recognition of error. 'Stings' invokes religious imagery (the metaphor of Mary Magdalene) in order to depict the speaker's sense of her role as subservient helpmeet to the bee master. Characteristically, though, this subservience is short-lived. In stanza seven we see the speaker gathering strength in order, like Lady Lazarus, to transcend the boundaries of her imprisonment. The last of the sequence, 'Wintering', is the poem with which Plath had planned to close *Ariel*. For Van Dyne, 'Wintering' should be read in the light of Plath's recently becoming a mother. More specifically, Plath 'takes the greatest risk in the sequence in associating the female body with nature'. Where 'Edge' (written on the reverse side of drafts of 'Wintering') traces the closing down of the maternal and creative body, 'Wintering' seems to 'struggle . . . in the opposite direction'.[12]

The best-known 'narrative rite of rebirth' in Plath's canon is, of course, 'Lady Lazarus' (*CP* 244). The poem presents a resurgent subject, rising, renewed, from the ashes. Interestingly, it also develops the theme of the double, implicitly encoded in the use of echoes, mirrors and other duplicating devices mentioned above. Stan Smith argues that in 'Lady Lazarus' 'the rapid shifts of the imagery enact the doubleness of a self which is a solid "opus", a "valuable", the "pure gold baby" of the collective patriarchy, and then, across an enjambment, "melts to a shriek"'.[13] 'Lady Lazarus' exemplifies the difficulty, raised earlier, of differentiating between the lived experience, emotions or voice of the poet and those of an invented speaker, or 'I'. Like the slightly earlier poem 'Daddy' (they were written two weeks apart in October 1962), 'Lady Lazarus' places that distinction under great strain. This is embodied by the urgency of voice in both poems, by the vividness of the imagery and by the metaphoric and symbolic intensity which make any supposed gap between biography and its representation seem highly suspect. In George Steiner's words, 'the vehemence and intimacy of the verse is such as to constitute a very powerful rhetoric of sincerity'.[14] The emphatic repetition of the 'I' sound, which, as in the earlier 'The Colossus', reverberates throughout is also significant. In 'Lady Lazarus' the 'I' is frequently carried over into internal rhymes ('smiling', 'like', 'nine', 'times', 'die' in stanza seven and 'annihilate' in stanza eight) with the effect that the 'I' seems desperately to be asserting voice and agency. 'Lady Lazarus' looks back to 'The Colossus' in other ways, too. The 'I'll never get it done' of the latter emerges as 'I've done it again' in the former.

Although it is common to read the voice of 'Lady Lazarus' as defiant and rebellious, one might counter by noting the flatness of its tone. At the very least, one might note the tension the poem establishes between the energy of the short, three-line stanzas (some lines containing only one or two words or two or three syllables – 'my knees', 'dying') and the lingering discontent of the longer and more complex lines. Where these appear, they detail the grounds for despair, attenuate and thereby dissipate the energetic anger, and slow the whole poem down. The frequent assonance has a similar effect. The long, slow vowel sounds and the repetition of key phrases ('I do it so it feels' and 'it's easy enough to do' in stanzas sixteen and seventeen respectively) ensure the reader's absorption in the scene. 'The Applicant' similarly apostrophises the reader, making them part of the relationship laid bare in the poem (*CP* 221).

The assumption of a confident and seductive salesperson's voice mimics the process by which ideology interpellates the subject in modern consumer culture. The stultifying rhymes, half-rhymes and internal rhymes ('crutch', 'crotch'; 'missing', 'thing'; 'proof', 'roof') and the flat repetitions ('hand', 'hand'; 'it', 'it'; 'that', 'that') exemplify the claustrophobia of the situation and the impossibility of breaking free or of refusing to be 'one of us'.

Critics have read 'Lady Lazarus' and 'The Applicant' as exposing the artifice of modern femininity, though in the case of 'The Applicant' it is the male addressee who is forced into a social straitjacket (represented by the 'black and stiff' suit of stanza five). 'Lady Lazarus' looks more specifically at the construction and distortion of female subjectivity. It depicts the fragmentation of the female body whose dismemberment brings to mind the story of Diana and Actaeon – again from Ovid's *Metamorphoses* (Actaeon is torn apart by his own hounds as punishment for having attempted to see what should have remained unseen). Lady Lazarus's 'big strip tease' (stanza ten) is, significantly, enforced by others. Although she assumes the voice of defiant bravado, it is others ('them') who 'unwrap' her. Thus she is coerced into performing, while seeming to authorise and enjoy, a spectacular femininity. Others have seen 'Lady Lazarus' as an allegory of a psychotherapeutic return through successive stages to some point of origin – a process which is dominated by 'Herr Doktor' who is also 'Herr Enemy' – or as another attempt to negotiate the relationship between self and father, self and husband, and self and patriarchy in general (hence 'Herr God' and 'Herr Lucifer' in the final lines). It is also possible to argue that 'Lady Lazarus' sounds an early note of caution about the direction which Plath's work, along with that of other confessional poets of her time, seemed to be taking. Plath expresses misgivings about the commodification of suffering (the 'charge', the 'very large charge') and the exploitation and self-exploitation which seem to underpin the mode.

'Lady Lazarus' has become so important in Plath's oeuvre perhaps because it allows readers coming from quite opposite theoretical positions to reach the same conclusions for different reasons. To quote Jacqueline Rose's summary of the situation:

> The concept of an emergent female selfhood . . . has been so crucial in a reading of these late poems. It is a reading which . . . is strangely shared by one form of feminist criticism and by Ted Hughes. What the two have in common is an image of transcendence – poetic, psychological, political – in which Plath finally takes off from, burns herself out of, whatever it was (false self for Hughes, Hughes himself for feminism) that had her in its thrall.[15]

However, as she goes on to say, this is a problematic reading for a number of reasons. It views Plath's oeuvre exclusively in terms of its relationship to the final poems and it overlooks the extent to which images of dissolution, self-effacement and abjection signify the impossibility ever of achieving the kind of subjectivity optimistically identified by some. As this indicates, 'Lady Lazarus' is not only, if at all, a personal complaint, or a suicide note *avant la lettre*. It also encodes broader commentaries on creativity and subjectivity in a social and political context. 'Lady Lazarus', like 'Daddy', the poem we move on to consider now, reflects on the lessons for modern civilisation of the Nazi Holocaust and other traumatic events.

Steiner was one of the first critics to comment on Plath's engagement with this theme and his views are generally sympathetic: 'Sylvia Plath had no personal, immediate contact with the world of the concentration camps . . . But her last, greatest poems culminate in an act of identification, of total communion with those tortured and massacred.' The relics in 'Lady Lazarus' (the 'cake of soap', the 'wedding ring' and 'gold filling') are more than the residue of one failed marriage, or even of a despairing femininity, they are among the poignant traces of the massacre of millions of Jews and others in the Nazi death camps. These 'notorious shards', as Steiner terms them, 'seemed to enter into her own being'.[16] For Steiner, a work of art such as Plath's poem is a crucial way of witnessing to the memory of the Holocaust.

Other readers, most notably Irving Howe, have objected to this identification, describing the allusions in 'Lady Lazarus' and 'Daddy' as 'illegitimate'. As he goes on to say, 'there is something monstrous, utterly disproportionate, when tangled emotions about one's father are deliberately compared with the historical fate of the European Jews; something sad, if the comparison is made spontaneously'.[17] Of 'Daddy', the critic Leon Wieseltier observes that 'the Jews with whom she identifies were victims of something worse than "weird luck". Whatever her father did to her, it could not have been what the Germans did to the Jews. The metaphor is inappropriate.'[18] James E. Young defends Plath's position and indicates that she was not alone in her use of Holocaust imagery. The subtle difference, as he puts it, is that where others wrote about the Holocaust explicitly from the outside, she internalises and reproduces motifs, images and memories which were part of the collective consciousness or cultural memory of her time: 'In Plath's case, her metaphors are built upon the absorption of public experience by language itself, experience that is then internalized and made private by the poet, used to order her private world, and then reexternalized in public verse.'[19] For Rose, what is at stake in these poems is the nature of representation itself. Howe, Wieseltier and others object to Plath's use of the Holocaust as a metaphor, whereas for Rose 'in the case of Plath, the question of metaphor brings with it – is inextricable from – that of fantasy and identification'. The issue, she argues, is 'not whether Plath has the right to represent the Holocaust, but what the presence of the Holocaust in her poetry unleashes, or obliges us to focus, about representation as such'. In her defence of 'Daddy', she explains that she sees the poem as a contemplation of its own 'conditions of linguistic and phantasmic production. Rather than casually produce an identification, it asks a question about identification, laying out one set of intolerable psychic conditions under which such an identification with the Jew might take place.'[20]

'Daddy' was written on 12 October 1962 (*CP* 183). Plath's own description of the poem, prepared for a BBC broadcast, identifies the voice as that of a 'girl with an Electra Complex' whose 'father died while she thought he was God'. The situation, she explains, is complicated because the father 'was also a Nazi' while the mother may have been 'part Jewish'. The daughter represents the embodiment of these tensions and contradictions and must 'act out the awful little allegory' once more in order to be released from it (*CP* 293). The rapid metre and clanging rhymes ('do', 'you', 'blue', 'du', 'two', 'Jew', 'goo', 'who' and so on) circle round and round in a claustrophobic movement which embodies the entrapment of the daughter. 'Daddy' is vast in scope and ambition. It is a transgressive poem which dares to think, and say, the inconceivable. It opens with a speaking self who resists incarceration in the 'black shoe' of habitual oppression. From this inauspicious beginning with its contradictory impulses towards action ('do') and stasis ('not') we move rapidly outwards, addressing the 'Daddy' of the title who, Colossus-like, now spans the whole nation. 'Daddy' shifts backwards and forwards in time in a hallucinatory motion which takes the poem away from the more documentary mode of, say, 'Electra on Azalea Path' and into the realm of the abstract. The poem explores themes of power and powerlessness, specifically as these are manifested in the daughter's search for a father who both must be killed, and is already dead. This powerlessness emerges in the poem as a supreme failure of communication – and thus as the ultimate exemplification of one of the keynotes of the whole collection. If it is the German language which prevents the subject's recovery of her father, then the strategy of figuring herself as Jewish (and therefore, as the World War II enemy of the Germans) helps both to explain and to exaggerate the daughter's plight. It is her difference from the father which puts her at fault and, in the terms of the poem, justifies her exile to 'Dachau, Auschwitz, Belsen'. From being treated as a victim, it is a small step to identifying herself as one.

In lines which have been troubling for many readers, especially feminist critics, the speaker embraces this identification of self as victim, becoming, in stanza ten, an apparently unashamed masochist. The bravado claim that 'every woman adores a Fascist' arguably undermines itself by its own hyperbole.

Throughout the poem, the speaker remains, at bottom, passive. She is the victim, the failure, the one destined for the camps. Even the ostensibly active part of killing the father is a role imposed on her rather than self-chosen, hence the curiously passive syntax of the line 'I have had to kill you' (stanza two). It is only in the final line that the speaker manages to break free of the figurative prison of the opening stanza. In a deeply ambiguous closing line, the speaker declares 'I'm through'. Rather as in the closing line of 'Medusa' (ostensibly addressed to Plath's mother, Aurelia), the syntax invites at least two contradictory readings (*CP* 224). 'I'm through' might mean that, at last, the barriers to communication have been breached and the speaker can now establish dialogue with the father. Alternatively, 'I'm through' connotes a final declaration of despair. The speaker, if 'through', has presumably had enough and is ready to abandon the struggle. 'Medusa', which ends 'there is nothing between us', again signals either a triumphant confirmation of the collapse of previous boundaries, or a newfound communion, or a final admission that there is no possible relationship – no shared ground to join 'us'. The poems leave all these possibilities open.

'Words' and 'Edge' are arguably two of Plath's finest works (*CP* 270, 272). Language is put to the test in the former, and stripped to the bone in the latter. In 'Words' (mentioned in Chapter 3), language figures simultaneously as a force for life (the ringing woods, the 'sap', the 'water') and as the source of death (hence the 'white skull'). The poem teaches the speaker that language is not, the first line notwithstanding, a tool or weapon which she can wield as she wishes. It is out of her control (a 'riderless horse'). Van Dyne points out that the speaker is effaced from this poem from the outset. Her scrutiny of Plath's worksheets shows that the only 'I' in the poem appeared quite late in the drafting process. The effect of this 'delayed entrance' is that it 'problematically situates the poet as only the latest in a string of uncontrollable consequences'.[21]

'Edge' was written just a few days later. In these 'drastically pared-down stanzas', as Britzolakis describes them, language – and the subjectivity it constitutes – are distilled to essentials. All that is left is the 'dead', the 'bare' and the 'empty'. This diminishing movement is exemplified in the form of the poem; eight of the ten two-line stanzas have a long opening line, followed by a falling shorter one. Yet against the odds, something does remain. Although it is common to read this poem as deadly and nihilistic (for Karen Jackson Ford, ' "Edge" kills off Plath the woman')[22] one might equally argue that there is a resurgent life force here. In the final four stanzas, life unexpectedly and uncannily moves, speaks and acts in the guise of the bleeding roses, the scented night flowers and the staring moon. Britzolakis adds that the image of the perfect dead woman may indeed be only an image: 'It is, after all, "the *illusion* of a Greek necessity".'[23]

Ariel: The Restored Edition

Which, then, are the key poems of Plath's original arrangement of *Ariel* that were omitted from the first (UK 1965/US 1966) edition? A number of important poems, as we will see in the next section, were moved into the posthumous collection *Winter Trees* (1971). Others were first collected in the 1981 *Collected Poems* and are restored in Plath's original order in the 2004 *Ariel: The Restored Edition*.

A tone of secrecy and suspicion characterises these omitted poems. 'A Secret' was written on 10 October 1962, within days of other key *Ariel* poems – 'The Applicant' and 'Daddy' (*A Rest* 198–200; *CP* 219). It offers a grotesque take on related themes – female subjectivity, femininity under surveillance (in 'A Secret' femininity is under constant scrutiny, is perpetually at fault), fertility, family, forms of revelation, leakage or betrayal. Here, as in 'The Courage of Shutting-Up' (another of Plath's original *Ariel* poems removed for later publication in *Winter Trees*), secrets are written on the body: 'stamped on you,/Faint, undulant watermark'. The addressee, then, gives secrets away without actually voicing them.

The anger and frustration of 'A Secret' are revealed in the close rhyme words whose energy and intensity is compacted in each successive stanza: 'blue', 'two', 'you', 'true', 'fool', 'roosting', 'cooing', 'you, you' and 'do' (the sequence anticipates the 'you'/'do' rhymes of 'Daddy'). There are several voices here (what Tracy Brain calls a 'Greek chorus') with snatches of reported dialogue reminiscent of the Lil and Albert section of T. S. Eliot's *The Waste Land* (1922).[24] Thus it is never entirely clear on whose conversation the reader is eavesdropping. Nevertheless, the oracular first person speaker who declares in stanza two 'I have one eye, you have two' seems to possess an insight that her addressee lacks. She is able to read the traces, to decode the signs. Alternatively, of course, we might read her 'one eye' as evidence – as with the Cyclops of Homer's *The Odyssey* – of imperfect vision and as a sign that she has been maimed and tricked. The reported dialogue, rhetorical questions, exclamations and emphatic repetitions thrust the reader into the middle of a heated debate. As the poem becomes increasingly surreal, chaotic and disjointed, our own certainty about what we are seeing and hearing becomes impaired. The poem is all the more effective for keeping its own secrets. As readers, we end up desperately wanting to identify what the secret is in the hope that this insight will somehow lend coherence to the whole.

In contrast to 'A Secret', 'The Jailer' seems to speak uncomfortably directly (*CP* 226). The first person voice outlines the background and conditions of her incarceration. Metaphor seems inadequate to the task of representing the scene, and the speaker falls back on bald description. Indeed, imagination or fantasy become, themselves, grounds for punishment. In stanza six, when the speaker admits to her dreams, she is punished for 'this subversion'. In this Bluebeard-like torture chamber (the speaker has been 'Hung, starved, burned, hooked'), she is trapped by her jailer's masochistic need of her. His identity, it seems, depends on her imprisonment. What, the final line asks, would he 'Do, do, do without me?' Again, the line recalls the rhyme and rhythm of 'Daddy' (written five days earlier) and its final admission of mutual, if violent, need.

Hughes justified his omission of certain poems from his edition of *Ariel* on the grounds of their personal aggression (*CP* 15). 'The Jailer' clearly falls into that group. It is possible to read the poem without recourse to biographical specificities – the relationship it explores is the symbiotic one between brutal guard and vulnerable prisoner. However, some of the details and nuances of the poem invite a different approach. Bundtzen, for example, identifies the speaker as Plath and, implicitly, the jailer with Hughes. Citing Rose's argument about the relationship between the abject body and language, she suggests, 'The boundaries between textual bodies and physical bodies here are so "worked over" that even when the only body "put at risk" appears to be Plath's own, she ends the poem by asking what her husband would do without her body to consume and dismember.' As we will see shortly, Bundtzen's question reflects Plath's use of the ancient mythological story of Philomela in 'The Courage of Shutting-Up'. The writer Robin Morgan goes further than Bundtzen in specifically indicting Hughes as Plath's jailer. In her notorious poem 'The Arraignment', she accuses Hughes of 'torture and murder'.[25] Such a strategy risks reducing the poems to mere witness statements and ignores the larger processes of fantasy which the text itself seeks to defend.

Two slightly earlier poems, 'Words heard, by accident, over the phone' (July 1962) and 'Burning the Letters' (August 1962) anticipate some of the concerns of 'A Secret' and 'The Jailer' – specifically the anxiety about forms of knowledge and failures of communication (*CP* 202, 204). Neither was included in Plath's *Ariel*; both appeared for the first time in the limited edition *Pursuit* of 1973 (*Bib* 38). In 'Words heard' an intercepted telephone call penetrates the security of the speaker's home, body and mind. The telephone extrudes a 'tentacle' which, like the 'eely tentacle' of 'Medusa', metaphorically embeds itself in its prey, paralysing her with its sting and then autotomising (or casting off a part of its self) in order to effect an escape. Here the spawn is left to 'percolate' in the speaker's heart. For Ford, this poem is not only about a real event, it is about language in the abstract. The poem begins in passive overhearing (and thus with the speaker in the position of object) but then transforms this into active representation (with the speaker assuming the role of subject).[26]

'Burning the Letters' also speaks eloquently of the painful acquisition of unwanted information. For Bundtzen, these two poems 'come alive especially when the biographical context is fully restored', yet one might argue that 'Burning the Letters' in particular is highly suggestive without this extratextual exegesis. The trajectory of the poem moves from a rather accepting, blank description of the speaker's deeds to a final fierce outcry. The opening stanza appropriates a colloquial tone with plentiful enjambment as though trying to normalise the speaker's actions ('well, I was tired'). The final stanza displays frequent end-stopping, harsh alliteration, exclamation marks and ellipses, all of which break up the flow of language and convey the impression of intense emotion. The speaker's attempt to obliterate the letters (to suppress the evidence) serves only to displace that knowledge. The truth will out, emerging in the final stanza in the fragments of a name rising, like some dreadful phoenix, from the ashes.

A final poem which Plath had planned to publish in *Ariel* but which was carried over into *Winter Trees* is 'Amnesiac' (*CP* 232). Written on 21 October 1962, this was originally a longer, two-part poem. It was only in November of that year, when *The New Yorker* opted to take just the second part, that Plath separated the two, calling the first part 'Lyonnesse' and the second 'Amnesiac'.[27] These poems contemplate the horror of loss, disappointment and creative collapse signalled rather more violently and acutely in the poems cited above. As Susan Bassnett points out, 'in Arthurian legend the kingdom of Lyonnesse was a mythical, ideal place off the coast of Cornwall. Here it is used as a symbol for something beautiful and lost that can never be recovered.'[28] Both parts of the poem open with the phrase 'no use', both employ an apparently restrained third person voice, and both proceed, in taut three-line stanzas reminiscent of Plath's earlier work, to catalogue a variety of things which have now gone. In 'Amnesiac' the subject tries to turn his back on history (to 'smooth' out traces of 'name, house, car keys'). In 'Lyonnesse' history returns with a vengeance.

Winter Trees and other late poems

In his carefully phrased explanation cum defence of his editorial policy in the years after Plath's death, Hughes outlines the contents of *Winter Trees*. It contains 'all but about six of the *Ariel* and after poems that were not in *Ariel*'. In other words, it includes poems that Plath wrote after she considered *Ariel* to be closed (*WP* 168). More confusingly, it includes poems which were very clearly part of Plath's original arrangement for *Ariel* ('Purdah' and 'Lesbos', for example) and the UK edition includes poems which had previously formed part of the original US edition of *Ariel*. Hughes's prefatory note to the English edition of *Winter Trees* explains that it includes some poems 'out of the batch from which the *Ariel* poems were more or less arbitrarily chosen' (*WT* 7). Hughes's ambivalence about the contents of this book and the earlier, posthumous *Crossing the Water* is clear. He worries that he may have 'compromised her best work' in preparing it for publication (*WP* 168–9).

For others, though, the poems of *Winter Trees* play an important role in consolidating the concerns of earlier works, or in suggesting new directions – both thematic and stylistic – in which Plath might have proceeded to travel. For Smith, for instance, 'Winter Trees' (the title poem) confirms an interest which dates back to 'The Manor Garden' (the opening poem of her first collection) in its exploration of the relationship between history and place: ' "Winter Trees" places history at the centre of a landscape where the graphic and defined emerges from the indefinite and obscure, and dawn vies with dissolution, growth and propagation with decline and denial.'[29] Many of the images recall the key poems of *Ariel* and earlier; the omniscient but curiously powerless trees, rooted to the spot yet unable to act ('easing nothing', as the final line of 'Winter Trees' puts it), remind us of 'Elm'. Yet these winter trees earn the envy of the woman speaker who sees in their inanimation precisely the kind of distancing from humanity's problems that she desires. More properly, the trees on the horizon deliver a sense of perspective and proportion. It is not, in fact, that they remain dissociated from the human world, it is that they put private concerns ('abortions', 'bitchery') into their true context. 'Waist-deep in history', as the final line of stanza two puts it, they see above and beyond the immediate and local, offering a reassuring sense of the bigger picture. The soft sibilance throughout the poem, the repeated 'ess' sounds and the internal rhymes ('leaves', 'ease') lend a mournful intensity to the poem's attempt to find reassurance in the external world (*CP* 257).

The speaking voice itself is curiously elided. There is an implicit observer but no identifiable speaker. In this respect, the poem invites comparison with just a small number of others in the collection which also eschew the first person, or indeed any single or coherent subject position. These include 'The Courage of Shutting-Up', drafted on 2 October 1962 (*CP* 209). Bundtzen observes that it was only from the third typed draft onwards that Plath revised the title: 'from "The Courage of Quietness" from what is often conceived of as a feminine virtue to the internalization of what is usually a command by another'.[30] The poem opens with a line which conjures up the horror of the moment before a firing squad or the threat of torture (perhaps the moment before the electric chair is switched on, to look back to the opening of *The Bell Jar* (1963)). What courage it takes, the poem asserts, to stay silent under the threat of such violence. The silence of the shut mouth masks the active assimilation of the truth which is quietly, discreetly, being recorded (hence 'black disks' and 'lined brain') – perhaps as ammunition or evidence for future conflicts. There is an implicit reference here – brought into the open in stanza four's reference to the 'dangerous' tongue which must be excised – to the mythological story of Philomela from Ovid's *Metamorphoses*.

Philomela is tricked and then raped by her sister Procne's husband, Tereus. When she protests Tereus violently cuts out her tongue to stop her proclaiming the truth of her violation. As Ovid explains, 'grief and pain breed great ingenuity, and distress teaches us to be inventive', and Philomela sets to work weaving a representation of her plight on a tapestry. This is then secretly delivered to Procne. She, too, is silenced by the knowledge she acquires. Later, though, she rescues Philomela and the two of them wreak their revenge in the most painful and violent way possible – by killing Procne's and Tereus's son and feeding the unwitting Tereus the body.[31] Geoffrey Hartman discusses the story in his essay 'The Voice of the Shuttle' and suggests that its fundamental meaning is that 'truth will out'.[32] In Plath's hands the story becomes a narrative of desire, deception and protest. Resistance can take many forms. Denied the power of speech (because of the loss of her tongue or because of language's inadequacy), Philomela and her sister turn to the language of the body; their gestures speak more effectively than words. Stanzas two and three of Plath's poem, which introduce the figure of the surgeon, develop this point. The surgeon's role is ambiguous; he is implicit in the mutilation of the speaker yet at the same time it is precisely this mutilation (the tattooing of the body) which gives metaphorical voice to the subject's trauma.

Deborah Nelson reads 'The Courage of Shutting-Up' as figuring the tension in the immediate Cold War period in which it was written between the pressure to remain silent and the contradictory imperative to disclose and reveal – specifically to betray those accused, in some nebulous way, of un-American activities: 'The surgeon in "The Courage of Shutting-Up" forces internal secrets to light by tattooing "blue grievances" on the surface of the skin . . . the surgeon makes a living by breaching the surface of the body.' As she goes on to argue, 'In so many of these poems – "A Secret", "Purdah", "The Detective", "Eavesdropper", "The Other", "The Jailer", "Words heard, by accident, over the phone", "The Courage of Shutting-Up" – there are irresistible pressures to tell secrets.' Again, the broad, ideological context is invaluable. It supplements, without supplanting, the biographical circumstances, too – the sense of vulnerability, suspicion and betrayal which a young wife and mother might experience on the bitter collapse of her idealised marriage. Like Nelson, Tim Kendall reads the poem in terms of betrayal, though he sees the real traitor as not the surgeon, but the dead man (father? husband?) in the mirror of the penultimate stanza.

However, we need to consider what happens immediately before this when the speaker looks in the mirror and sees – presumably – her own reflection ('the eyes, the eyes, the eyes'). What she learns is that although one can forgo verbal utterance (or possess the courage of shutting-up), one's eyes cannot disguise the truth of what they have seen. The dismayed fading away in the final stanza, with its sequence of negatives ('no', 'no longer', 'insolvent'), and falling rhythms (the trochees of 'pigeons' and 'mountains') represents her final self-surrender.[33]

Other poems in *Winter Trees* employ the far more personal and immediate voice we will recognise from *Ariel*. Most famous, and perhaps most notorious, among these is 'The Rabbit Catcher', which was included in Plath's arrangement for *Ariel* but taken out by Hughes. Middlebrook points to associations between Plath's poem, D. H. Lawrence's poem 'Rabbit Snared in the Night' and Hughes's story 'Harvesting'. In turn, Hughes's poem 'The Rabbit Catcher' (in *Birthday Letters* (1998)) reinterprets, and responds to, all three sources.[34] Like 'The Courage of Shutting-Up', 'The Rabbit Catcher' opens with a moment of violence: 'It was a place of force –.' The closing en-dash works in several ways: it allows time for the point to sink in; it implies that the force is sudden and ongoing, and that the speaker's utterance has been interrupted by it. Rather as in 'Blackberrying', the speaker feels herself to be enclosed, almost asphyxiated (hence the gagged mouth of stanza two), within the confines of a narrow chasm or funnel. Traps and snares perform the work of the 'hooks' seen elsewhere in Plath's work and represent the demands and restraints of domesticity. The thrill or charge which these 'little deaths' bring (the term 'little death' conventionally connotes male orgasm) gestures towards an unsettlingly sadomasochistic relationship between hunter and prey and recalls the dynamic of 'The Jailer' and the lines from 'Daddy' wherein 'Every woman adores a Fascist'. The final stanza of 'The Rabbit Catcher' sounds a terrible warning. The awful implication – reified in the rabbit-snare mechanism – is that the more one struggles against violence or oppression, the tighter one is trapped in it. Passivity (or the 'courage of shutting-up') becomes the only option, even though it is an option which promises no escape. Rose's lengthy and detailed analysis of this poem reads it as an exploration of 'the play of gender, sexuality and power'. More specifically, it forces (I use the word intentionally) a recognition of the potential relationships between desire, fantasy, violence and sexual identity.[35]

Three Women

In addition to 'The Rabbit-Catcher', the major single work in *Winter Trees* is *Three Women: A Poem for Three Voices* (*CP* 176). Described by Steven Gould

Axelrod as one of Plath's 'important social poems' it 'reflects on the dilemmas of women's bodies and choices in a masculinist society'. The poem was written in March 1962 as a drama script for BBC Radio and broadcast in September of that year. In a letter to her mother, Plath notes that one of its influences is 'a Bergman film' (*LH* 456) which Bundtzen later identified as *Brink of Life* (1958). Middlebrook sees the drafting of this work, which Plath undertook after the birth of her second child, as a symbolic alignment on Plath's part with the experiences and voices of the unnamed women in the poem and as a turn away from the male mentors with whom she had previously identified.[36] The concern with questions of voice and voicelessness, with male medical authority (see 'The Courage of Shutting-Up' and 'The Surgeon at 2 a.m.'), with the female body, female creativity and female agency, is coherent with other poems in *Winter Trees*. These include the ambivalent blessing of 'Child', the satirical 'Gigolo', the defiant 'Purdah' with its resounding 'shriek' of identity wrested from oppression, and the close of 'The Rabbit-Catcher'. The exposé of a femininity which is medicalised or pathologised but nevertheless familiar and unexpectedly seductive is also in keeping with some of the stories and sketches from *Johnny Panic and the Bible of Dreams* and with moments from *The Bell Jar*.

Three Women opens with the 'first voice' – that of a woman who, it transpires, is glad to be a mother. She situates herself at the centre of the world – as a kind of Omphalos around which everything else circles. The poem invokes a by now familiar metaphor for femininity and fertility – the moon. Yet the speaker's creativity seems to have emerged in spite of the moon, which is here a mere observer, astonished by, and dissociated from, what the first voice has achieved in her own right (line 7). The 'second voice' (the voice of the woman who miscarries her baby) assimilates images of cold, rational masculinity (the code of 'abstractions') as a counterpoint to the rich creativity whose failure or loss the speaker mourns. Similar motifs, used more specifically of the struggle to sustain poetic creativity, appear in poems such as 'Stillborn'. In stanza two of her speech, the cold, echoing tapping of the typewriter keys simultaneously suggests a metonym for writing and demonstrates just how flat and inadequate is this sublimation of the desire to create. The 'third voice' (the voice of a woman who gives her unwanted child away) implicitly figures pregnancy as a symptom of violation. The 'great swan' which threatens the speaker recalls the ancient Greek story of Leda's rape by Zeus in the guise of a swan. Plath's reference to the 'snake in swans' encodes both the phallic threat and the treachery of Zeus's deception.

Throughout the poem, Plath is able to distinguish and explore the entirely different experiences and perspectives of the three women. However, when it was first broadcast on BBC radio 'two of the three readers engaged for the production were, at almost the last moment, unable to take part, and had to be replaced at short notice; consequently the voices of the three women were not differentiated as clearly as they should have been.' Nevertheless, Douglas Cleverdon, the radio producer who broadcast the piece, commends its 'simple but dramatic' effectiveness, and its deployment of a 'visualizing imagination, dramatically expressed in clear and speakable language'.[37] Significantly, Plath does not name the women – referring to them only as 'first', 'second' and 'third' voices and allowing them subtly to reveal their circumstances. Nevertheless, it has been common to label the three as 'wife', 'secretary' and 'student'. The effect of Plath's nondisclosure of the precise identities of the three women is to demonstrate the diversity of female experience and the equal validity of each of the routes open to them. Alternatively, we might say that the poem illustrates the lack of agency of each of these women who are, in fact, unable to choose any particular route and must merely respond in the best way they can to the particular circumstances in which their gender and sexuality places them. Middlebrook suggests that the 'three voices may well be semi-conscious emanations of Plath's disquiet regarding the emotional figuration that had developed after her own miscarriage and the birth of Nicholas'.[38] Although this particular situation may well be the starting point, the poem rapidly moves beyond the personal and immediate and into a broader articulation of women's relationships to their bodies, their fertility and medical practice at this time.

'Lesbos' also explores the experience of women's lives, this time with an emphasis on the oppressive rituals of the everyday or the world of the 'modern streamlined wife', as Perloff puts it (*CP* 227).[39] As Chapters 1 and 2 showed, Plath's poems emerged in a culture which valorised the suburban domestic home as the heart of a secure nation and the natural environment for an idealised femininity:

> The family home would be the place where a man could display his success through the accumulation of consumer goods. Women, in turn, would reap rewards for domesticity by surrounding themselves with commodities. Presumably, they would remain content as housewives because appliances would ease their burdens. For both men and women, home ownership would reinforce aspirations for upward mobility and diffuse [*sic*] the potential for social unrest.[40]

'Lesbos' exposes and explodes this ideal. The relentlessly end-stopped lines spit out a catalogue of anger, resentment and despair. Children, animals, husband and self – all are bitterly indicted. All are in disarray – mixed up, as Marsha

Bryant notes, with the accoutrements of modern suburban life (the fluorescent lights, staticky radio and sleeping pills) to form a kind of 'domestic surreal': 'Plath does not simply transform the dream kitchen into a nightmare. Ariel's kitchen opens up domesticity . . . but adds an intensity charged by strange combinations of housewifery with the supernatural and mechanical.'[41]

Chapter 5

The Bell Jar and Johnny Panic and the Bible of Dreams

The Bell Jar

For some early critics, Sylvia Plath's 1963 novel, *The Bell Jar*, was best thought of as 'a poet's notebook' or as 'a poet's novel, a casebook almost in stanzas'.[1] More recent commentators have seen it as more than mere apprentice work for the later poetry. Elizabeth Wurtzel commends its 'remarkable achievement' and describes it as 'very funny, smartly detached, and often nasty in a voice too honest to be unsympathetic', while Robin Peel notes its 'wonderfully mordant humour'.[2]

The difficulty of assessing the literary merit of *The Bell Jar* is compounded by its complicated publishing history. It was first published in England by Heinemann on 14 January 1963 under the pseudonym that Plath had chosen, Victoria Lucas. Diane Middlebrook explains that the decision to use a pseudonym was partly influenced by the apparently autobiographical nature of some of the material in the book; the false name afforded a degree of disguise and protection. But she also speculates that it shows Plath's intention to establish an entirely separate – potentially more commercially successful – authorial persona, one that would appeal to a popular audience and not be confused with the persona behind the other, more highly valued, poetic work. According to Jacqueline Rose, the task for Plath was to 'engage in popular writing without detriment to – without violating – the purity of her art'.[3] Plath is reported as referring to the book as a 'potboiler' – and some critics have suggested that the uncertainty about when exactly it was written, discussed in more detail below, is evidence of her insecurity about working in this less esteemed genre.[4] The actual choice of nom-de-plume is also worthy of scrutiny. Peel indicates that Plath first considered the name 'Frieda Lucas' and titled the book *Diary of a Suicide*. Vance Bourjaily gives *The Girl in the Mirror* as a provisional title.[5]

A consequence of the decision to use the pseudonym is that the novel seems almost, like its heroine Esther Greenwood, to have been 'born twice' – or 'retreaded', as the closing lines of the book have it (*BJ* 257). On its UK emergence, it received a smattering of applause, achieved reasonable sales and then disappeared from view.[6] When the book was reissued in the UK three years after Plath's death and with her name on the cover, things began to look rather different. What had emerged in the interim was widespread news of Plath's death by suicide and key poems in numerous journals and newspapers. Most importantly, *Ariel* was published in March 1965 and June 1966 in the UK and USA respectively. As Middlebrook explains:

> Suddenly, Plath was marketable on both sides of the Atlantic. As a consequence of this flurry, Plath's British publisher, Faber, brought out a new edition of *The Bell Jar* in September 1966, identifying the author as Sylvia Plath for the first time; between 1966 and 1977, Faber sold over 140,000 copies of *The Bell Jar* in hardback and paperback editions.[7]

Wurtzel's characteristically acerbic commentary on the situation confirms Middlebrook's reading:

> The novel by unknown 'Victoria Lucas' was rejected out of hand by Knopf – the American company that published Plath's poetry was baffled that they'd even received such an objectionable submission by a complete unknown talent from Heinemann – and editor William Koshland wrote that he was 'knocked galley west' to discover that the true author was Plath. Koshland explained that he and his colleagues at Knopf felt it was just a typical first novel that the poet had to 'get out of her system,' and that it read 'as if it were autobiographical, flagrantly so'; Harper & Row, which would ultimately publish *The Bell Jar* in 1971, rejected it first because 'the story ceases to be a novel and becomes case history.'[8]

From 1965 in particular, the novel has been read in the knowledge – or more properly perhaps with a thirst for knowledge – of the lived experience of the author. It has been read with a view to the insights it might offer into the working processes of the poet, and as though this were the real, authentic voice of the now-dead author communicating from beyond the grave. Second time round, it was met with a chastened response from a hitherto neglectful readership. As

M. L. Rosenthal confesses, 'I very much regret missing [the novel in 1963] for now it is impossible to read without thinking of [Plath] personally and of the suicidal poems in *Ariel*.'[9] Responses such as this indicate several of the main issues which arise when encountering *The Bell Jar*. The first is the matter of the relationship between Plath's own life and experience – specifically her time as an intern at *Mademoiselle* magazine in the summer of 1953, her subsequent suicide attempt and her hospitalisation – and the plot of the novel. Is *The Bell Jar* merely a thinly disguised report of real events? The second, which relates to this, is the question of the structure, narrative voice and complex texture of the novel (its use of specific metaphors and motifs – mirrors, mouths, babies, food, funnels or tunnels, costume and disguise and so on). How effective are these in structural and aesthetic terms? Even if we want to concede that the novel is best read as a meditation on, and mediation of, Plath's own past experiences, is that all it is? Does it offer the autobiography of a single subject or does it portray a broader picture of cultural and ideological life in 1950s white America? For Robert Scholes, it does all these things: '*The Bell Jar* is about the events of Sylvia Plath's twentieth year: about how she tried to die, and how they stuck her back together with glue. It is a fine novel, as bitter and remorseless as her last poems.' It is also, he goes on to say, 'about the way this country was in the Fifties and about the way it is to lose one's grip on sanity and recover it again'.[10]

If the publication and reception history of *The Bell Jar* are complicated, its date of origin seems equally problematic. Judith Kroll indicates that Plath was working on the book during January 1962. However, she also suggests that the manuscript had been completed some months earlier, citing a letter from Plath to her mother of 20 November 1961 in which she explains that even though she had recently received a Eugene F. Saxton writer's grant to help her compose a novel, the work itself was already done (*LH* 437). Kroll also cites the speculation of Plath's one-time biographer Lois Ames, that Plath may have ' "already had a version of *The Bell Jar* in her trunks when [in 1957] she returned to the States" '.[11] Peel argues that the book was 'produced during the spring and summer of 1961 . . . it was complete by the time they moved to Devon in August'. Middlebrook narrows it down further still, proposing that Plath worked on the draft between March and May of that year, and that 'it took her only six weeks'.[12] Hughes suggests February to May (*LTH* 536).

The uncertainty about when, exactly, the book was written makes it difficult to assert any clear contiguities between sections of the novel and specific poems written at the same time. Nevertheless, there are key works (notably 'Poem for a Birthday') whose composition, predating *The Bell Jar*, does indicate some of the seeds or roots of the novel's emergence. 'Poem for a Birthday', as we have seen, was written at the Yaddo writers' colony in late 1959. It is here that she encountered Theodore Roethke's textual engagement with themes of mental instability and treatment. This literary model, coupled with the return home after two years of university and marriage in England, may have nudged Plath to revisit scenes from her past life. Tim Kendall sees connections between the voices of Plath's 1962 *Three Women: A Poem for Three Voices* and the identities assumed in *The Bell Jar*: 'The Bell Jar switches between three Esthers: the virgin, the sexually liberated, and the mother.' For Tracy Brain, 'Among the Narcissi' is an important reference point. Rather than suggesting that this April 1962 poem influences *The Bell Jar* (which, as we have seen, may well have been completed by this time), Brain usefully shows how the drafts of the novel influenced the poem. Her scrutiny of the Plath archives identifies several deleted scenes, specifically some relating to the feminisation (and thus mockery) of Buddy Willard. She argues that the affectionate and sympathetic portrait of the old and infirm man in 'Among the Narcissi', drafted on the reverse side of excised pages from *The Bell Jar*, reveals a 'tolerance and compassion' in Plath that Esther Greenwood could not yet admit.[13] Brain's work (like Peel's, Middlebrook's, Susan Van Dyne's and Lynda K. Bundtzen's, among others) provides useful evidence, based on scholarly research in the archives, about the ongoing relationship between the two parts of Plath's oeuvre.

In addition to identifying these internal connections, it is helpful to look at other possible external influences. Steven Gould Axelrod and Brain read *The Bell Jar* in the light of Plath's reading of Charlotte Brontë and Virginia Woolf, respectively, while Gordon Lameyer points to the importance of Dostoevsky to the book.[14] Middlebrook draws attention to D. H. Lawrence's work, specifically his metaphor of the fig in *Women in Love* as one of the models for Plath's own fig metaphor, which in *The Bell Jar* represents Esther's paralysis when faced with a multitude of unreachable and indistinguishable opportunities. This metaphor plays a crucial role in the narrative. It emerges first in the guise of a story Esther reads when confined to bed after the *Ladies Day* lunch poisoning episode. The *Ladies Day* staff send a consolatory book with a Get Well card which Esther clearly finds ridiculous. It features a 'poodle in a flowered bed jacket sitting in a poodle basket with a sad face' (*BJ* 56). The defamiliarising voice which is so characteristic of the novel exposes the hidden message of the card – that the magazine's guest editors are themselves passive, decorative and mindless poodles. Esther opens her copy of the gift book, *The Thirty Best Stories of the Year*, and reads the story of the fig tree. In this first appearance the metaphor represents frustrated desire; two star-crossed lovers meet to collect figs under a tree until their plans are thwarted by a 'mean-faced' servant (*BJ* 57). Tellingly, it is not the romantic plot that attracts Esther's interest. What she is seduced by are the aesthetic qualities of the tree – its solidity and abundance. She wants to enter into this story, she says, to slip between the lines of text in order to find peace beneath the 'beautiful big green fig-tree'. Earlier still, Esther has chafed under the requirements of her college physics class, yearning instead for the living, breathing 'leaf shapes' of her previous botany course (*BJ* 36–7).

The fig tree motif emerges for the second time a little later when Esther pictures herself faced with numerous choices: the options of marriage and children; success as a poet, professor or editor; success in Europe, Africa or South America; success with one of a succession of men; or, more outlandishly, success as 'an Olympic lady crew champion' (*BJ* 80). Spoiled for choice, Esther is unable to make a choice. Her editor, Jay Cee, later says of Esther at a photo shoot during which the young women are required to dress up to demonstrate where they have come from and what they aspire to be: 'she wants . . . to be everything' (*BJ* 106). In the allegorical story that Esther imagines, the moment passes, the unpicked and now rotten figs fall from the tree, and she remains trapped in its branches, 'starving to death' (*BJ* 80). There are several points to make here. The first is that Esther, because she has to choose just one of these figs (or life choices) – each of which seems to cancel out the others – finds herself unable to do anything. Wurtzel reads this scene within the context of 1950s ideals of femininity: 'Plath', she argues (though one might wish to differentiate here between 'Plath' and her fictional creation, Esther), 'suffered from wanting so much in a world that did not allow women to want anything at all'.[15] The second point is that the images of self as starving because she is too greedy to select just one fig sustain a major concern in the novel – about need and satiety, excess and restraint. The reverse side of such metaphors, as we will see in a moment, emerges in images of evacuation, poison, sickness and bile.

The *Ladies Day* lunch which is the catalyst for the gift of the book sets in train a complex set of associations. Again and again, Esther refers to herself as 'starving' (*BJ* 25, 51, 191). Her enthusiastic and detailed descriptions of food and eating throughout the novel indicate the importance of food (and more broadly of satisfying her own physical desires) to her sense of self but also show her to be transgressing ideals of femininity: 'The rules for the constitution of femininity . . . require that women learn to feed others, not the self, and to construe any desires for self-nurturance and self-feeding as greedy and excessive.'[16] Esther is punished when the first awful sign of her impending second bout of ECT is heralded by the denial of food. After the ECT, Esther rewards herself with the longed-for breakfast egg – itself, of course, a symbol of new life and hope (*BJ* 222–3, 228). Throughout *The Bell Jar*, there is something simultaneously sexual and ritualistic about food and eating (*BJ* 27). Of Plath's 1962 story 'Mothers' (*JP* 106–16), whose protagonist is also called

Esther, Kendall notes, 'Esther seems intuitively aware that food is the shibboleth of social acceptance.'[17] It is also deeply divisive; appetite, taste and knowledge of the sometimes arcane rituals of the table separate those who have a right to be there from those who do not. This is true both of the world of the New York magazine, and, later, of the hierarchical spaces of the mental institution.

Narrative voice

The narrative voice of *The Bell Jar* is one of its greatest strengths. In the opening scene alone we have a voice which is simultaneously detached from what it sees and detached from itself but also wholly implicated. The first few paragraphs move from events of national – indeed global – import (the electrocution of Ethel and Julius Rosenberg who had been charged with betraying nuclear secrets to the Soviet Union) to the effect this has on the vulnerable self. Esther is physically sickened by news of the pair as, with all her senses, she assimilates their acute pain, finding herself overwhelmed by 'the peanut-smelling mouth of every subway' (*BJ* 2). The peanut image is no mere atmospheric detail. Later in the novel, peanuts are again associated with death when Esther helps herself to some peanuts from a bag she had bought as bird food (another sign of her punishable gluttony?) while reading a newspaper report of an attempted suicide and other violent acts (*BJ* 144; *J* 541–2).

The first paragraph sets up a tension between involvement (self-willed or enforced by others; the distinction is unclear) and dissociation. The Rosenberg case has 'nothing to do' with Esther, but nevertheless she persists in thinking about it. This establishes a pattern which recurs throughout the novel where Esther seems, in turn, separated from the world around her, separated from others (again and again, she returns to her difference from the other guest editors, other college girls, other family members, other mental patients) and, crucially, separated from herself. The fractured time frame of the novel helps to sustain this duplicity. The immediacy of the opening lines gives way to a much broader and long-term perspective as the protagonist looks back on past events. It is clear that she has survived the experience she has just introduced. As soon as she was 'all right again', she tells us (the shift to the present tense at this point is important in establishing a distance from what has gone before), she feels well enough to look at the material mementoes of her time at the New York magazine (*BJ* 3). Moreover, she now has a baby. This very obvious sign of conformity to the idealised feminine role common in mid-century America comes to seem startling in the light of the ostentatious disavowal of any interest in babies throughout the rest of the novel. Nevertheless, the theme of mothering (and, implicitly, the question of what makes a good mother) is an important one to which we will return.

The voice of *The Bell Jar* has often been compared to that of Holden Caulfield, the hero of J. D. Salinger's 1951 novel *The Catcher in the Rye*. For Charles Newman, the book is 'the record, in a strange blend of American and British vernacular, of a female Holden Caulfield driven to self-destruction by despair with the alternatives adult life apparently offers'.[18] But it might also be compared to the voice of Mark Twain's Huckleberry Finn, whose affectionate allusions to authorial 'stretchers' open his eponymous *Adventures* (1884). In like manner, the bravado and apparent honesty of the opening lines of *The Bell Jar* mask a less reliable narrator than at first appears. Much of the irony in the novel comes from the separation of the subject as narrator from the subject as participant (or the 'I' of the *énonciation* and the 'I' of the *énoncé* – the 'I' who is in the process of speaking and the 'I' who is spoken about). This allows Esther to obtain a degree of critical distance on her self and her world, and it constructs a space in which irony can flourish. It is often the case that in the guise of exposing others (for example, in chapter 11 where Esther describes her encounter with her first psychiatrist, Dr Gordon) she exposes herself (*BJ* 137). Brain's scrutiny of the drafts of *The Bell Jar* suggests that Plath intended her readers to distrust Esther's voice. She cites an excised passage where Esther admits to absorbing other people's life stories from wherever she managed to hear them (shades of the narrators of the stories 'Johnny Panic and the Bible of Dreams' and 'The Daughters of Blossom Street' here) and then confesses, ' "I never told anybody my life story, though, or if I did, I made up a whopper." '[19] As Brain concludes, 'these deleted passages indicate Plath's conception of her narrator as less than wholly reliable'.

The double

Plath's longstanding interest in the figure of the double has been noted before. *The Bell Jar* uses successive images of doubling in myriad ways. The opening scene alone, as we have seen, sets up a distinction between the Esther of then (that summer in New York) and the Esther of now (the mother figure who is looking back on the past). Ethel Rosenberg forms a kind of double to Esther. Deborah Nelson points out that Ethel's full name was Esther Ethel Greenglass Rosenberg, thus her maiden name, Esther Greenglass, offers an uncanny parallel to Esther Greenwood's. Both women, one might argue, suffer for their nonconformity to the feminine ideals which dominated Cold War America. Both are portrayed as outsiders or alien others. The horror of electrocution which dominates Esther's mind in these opening pages anticipates, and finds a double in, her subsequent ECT sessions. As Nelson says, 'In naming her heroine after a victim of hysterical anticommunism, [Plath] casts Esther's rebellion against 1950s codes of femininity in Cold War terms.'[20]

Rather as with the invocation of the Holocaust in some of the *Ariel* poems discussed in the previous chapter, this is a contentious analogy to make. Peel cites the critic Denis Donoghue's accusation that Plath's comparison of Esther's situation with that of the Rosenbergs is ' "blatant rather than just" '.[21] However, arguably, Plath's (or Esther's) telescoping of the personal and the national only mirrors the process by which the individual actions of the Rosenbergs were taken to have global import. In the words of the prosecuting attorney, 'We will prove that the Rosenbergs devised and put into operation . . . an elaborate scheme which enabled them to steal through David Greenglass this one weapon, that might well hold the key to the survival of this nation and means the peace of the world, the atomic bomb.'[22] Moreover, Ethel's crime, like Esther's, lies less in what she has done than in who she is. It is her interpretation (or misinterpretation) of femininity which is perceived to be at fault. Pat Macpherson cites President Eisenhower's explanation of his refusal to commute Ethel's death sentence:

> I must say that it goes against the grain to avoid interfering in the case where a woman is to receive capital punishment. Over against this, however, must be placed one or two facts that have greater significance. The first of these is that in this instance it is the woman who is the strong and recalcitrant character; the man is the weak one. She has obviously been the leader in everything they did in the spy ring.[23]

It was Ethel's alleged commitment to communism over her commitment to her children which seemed to confirm her malignancy and to justify her sentence. Esther's repeated disavowal of any maternal instincts and her obvious distaste for children suggests a replication of Ethel's perceived position. This is seen most clearly in chapter eighteen where Esther sits in a clinic waiting room before her appointment for the fitting of a contraceptive device. Here the sight of 'Eisenhower-faced babies' threatens to send her back into the world of the insane (*BJ* 234).

The Rosenberg analogy also throws up the theme of betrayal, a theme which reemerges in Esther's eyes in the actions of her second psychiatrist, Dr Nolan. She promises to tell Esther in advance if she plans to use ECT, then fails to fulfil the spirit of that promise by giving her only a few minutes' notice of what is about to happen (*BJ* 200, 223–4). It emerges, too, in the guise of the deception which Buddy Willard plays on her. He masquerades as a pure, wholesome and sexually inexperienced young man – thus as her equal – while actually having already slept with another woman (*BJ* 59).

In addition to Ethel Rosenberg, other women figure as doubles; first Esther's co-editors, Doreen and Betsy, then her boss, Jay Cee, then Dr Nolan – even her boyfriend's mother, Mrs Willard. Each in turn, like the figs on the fig tree, offers an alternative model of adult femininity. Which will Esther choose to emulate? There are other already rejected doubles, too: the mother and the mentor (Philomena Guinea, a thinly disguised portrait of Plath's mentor Olive Higgins Prouty). And there are male doubles: Constantin the 'simultaneous interpreter' and his 'negative double' Marco the violent predator.[24] The most important double, however, is Esther's mother – a dreadful double who implicitly bears a responsibility for Esther's fate. Mrs Greenwood hovers in the background of the novel, appearing only sporadically but always at times of great crisis. The oppressive, suffocating mother represents a form of living bell jar as she seeks to scrutinise and stifle her daughter's movements. Kroll implies a connection between the bell jar of the novel and the line from Plath's 'Medusa' which refers to 'your body/Bottle in which I live'.[25] The news Mrs Greenwood gives Esther of her failure to secure a place on the summer writing course to which she had applied is just one of these moments and is the catalyst for Esther's suicide attempt. Subsequently, she emerges to torment her daughter with her 'sorrowful face' and her appeals that Esther tell her 'what she had done wrong' (*BJ* 215). It is at this moment that Esther realises, and admits out loud, that she hates her mother – a confession which is one of the steps leading to her second bout of ECT and subsequent recovery. Locked in a terrible symbiotic relationship, it is as though the daughter can live only by killing off her mother/double (see *J* 543–6, 429–38).

Aurelia Plath was deeply distressed by the portrayal of the mother in *The Bell Jar*. In an essay ('Letter Written in the Actuality of Spring') published in Paul Alexander's *Ariel Ascending*, she expresses her views about the book, setting it in the context of contemporary ideologies of femininity, domesticity and family. *The Bell Jar* and a number of poems, she says ('The Disquieting Muses' is the example she gives), 'involve the mother figure as the whipping boy, so characteristic of the Fifties'. She describes the novel as 'a violation' and says of her daughter that 'through her creative process, she transformed personalities into cruel and false caricatures, misleading though artistically more convincing than the truth would be'.[26] Sympathetic though one might be to Aurelia's perspective, her misgivings about the book unwittingly offer a form of defence; it is precisely in its creativity, in its capacity to transform and to aestheticise, that its strength lies.

Brain offers a nuanced defence of the portrayal of Mrs Greenwood, suggesting that she is treated with rather more sympathy than might, at first, appear. She quotes an unpublished letter from Plath to her Heinemann editor wherein Plath describes Esther's mother as ' "a dutiful hard-working mother whose beastly daughter is ungrateful to her" '. Brain argues that 'we should not swallow uncritically Esther's angry perceptions of her mother'.[27] I concur with this reading; the mistreatment of the other is itself a measure of the narrator's egotism and solipsism. Esther is exposing her own self-absorption as much as condemning others. Nevertheless, Aurelia's unease – on her own part and on that of others who might identify themselves in the book – explains why it was not published in the USA until 1971. When it did appear, it was largely against Aurelia's, and even Ted Hughes's wishes, but a necessary response to copyright technicalities. The quid pro quo for this arrangement was, as the next chapter will explain, that Mrs Plath compile an edition of her daughter's *Letters Home.*[28]

To return to the figure of the double; another important 'other' to Esther is the character of Joan Gilling. Joan had been introduced earlier in the novel as one of Buddy Willard's dates and had been characterised as suspiciously masculine in interests and demeanour (*BJ* 61). She reappears unexpectedly in an adjacent room (a 'mirror image' of Esther's) in the same hospital wing (*BJ* 209). This is at a time when Esther is beginning to get better and is gradually moving her way up the ladder of hospital facilities, acquiring more and more privileges (shopping and cinema trips) as she proceeds (*BJ* 205). Joan's introduction heralds the end of this process, and a new decline in Esther (*BJ* 217). In this deadly competition, it seems that only one of the two women can win and Joan, like the mother, must be sacrificed to ensure Esther's survival.

It is after Esther's second round of ECT that she begins to leave her 'double' behind. With separation comes some recognition of the role each has played for the other. Esther comments that the two were so close that Joan's emotions 'seemed a wry, black image of my own'. Louis Simpson, quoting George Stade, suggests that Joan is 'a kind of disposal unit for traits that Sylvia Plath came to reject in herself'.[29] 'Sometimes,' as Esther goes on to say, 'I wondered if I had made Joan up' (*BJ* 231). The point is an important one which takes us back to the question raised earlier about the reliability of the narrator; we have only Esther's word to go on and this word is deeply suspect. There is a blatant precedent for this kind of duplicity in Esther's earlier self-avowed invention of an alter ego, Elly Higginbottom, in whom she invests aspects of the self that seem otherwise incongruous, or dangerous, or that she wishes to have the freedom to exercise. In chapter 2 Esther assumes the persona of Elly in order to go on a double-date with Doreen. Elly returns early to the hotel and is joined later by a drunken Doreen who bangs on her hotel door, calling ' "Elly, Elly, Elly" '. Doreen's voice is joined by that of the night maid calling, ' "Miss Greenwood, Miss Greenwood" '. As Esther comments, it was 'as if I had a split personality or something' (*BJ* 22).

In addition to the character doubles in the novel, many critics have found it productive to consider Plath herself as split. From this point of view, Esther is not an invented persona, but a voice which speaks from and for a part of Plath's own self. She serves the same function in respect to Plath as Joan does in respect to Esther. Bourjaily takes a similar line, seeing 'Victoria Lucas' as an aspect of Plath which she split off and assigned to a certain role, leaving 'Sylvia Plath' to concentrate on the real thing: *Ariel*.[30]

Subjectivity

Kroll reads *The Bell Jar* in terms of a battle between 'true' and 'false' selves.[31] Attractive though this interpretation is, it tends to reduce the novel to a binary system which the text itself rejects. The whole point for Esther is the inadequacy and instability of any such system of thought. Things are not what they seem – from the superficially enticing, ptomaine-stricken crab meat to the identity of Esther's friend, Joan – Esther's world is a mutable one where certainties about 'true' *vs.* 'false' selves are untenable. The unreliability of the narrator, the complex chronology of the book, and its wholly ambivalent ending, conspire against the temptation to see truth and certainty where there is only confusion and uncertainty. Esther's apparent success at the end is, surely, provisional. How do we (how does she?) know that the bell jar will not 'descend again?' (*BJ* 254). Esther's struggle throughout the novel is less to identify true or false selves than to feel or be anything at all. Repeatedly (and this is a trope we have seen in many of the poems) she sees herself as blank, faceless, featureless and mute. She experiences herself as out of place and experiences her body as alien or hostile or malfunctioning or in some way disconnected from her mind. Contemplating her futile and sometimes laughable attempts at suicide (Chapter 13), Esther concedes that her body 'had all sorts of little tricks' to keep it alive (*BJ* 169). In order to succeed, she will need to 'ambush it' as though it were some sort of alien other.

Esther's is not the only body in crisis. Throughout the novel, others respond to their circumstances with various forms of physical breakdown. Alongside the metaphors of food and consumption mentioned earlier are images of purgation and evacuation, vomiting and bleeding – from Betsy, Esther and the other guest editors' 'puking' in chapter 4 to the images of green bile, that season's 'in' colour in Chapter 9. In Chapter 11, shortly after Esther has read the newspaper stories about violent murders, suicides and muggings, her mind turns to Japan and what she understands to be the ritual whereby the Japanese 'disemboweled themselves when anything went wrong' (*BJ* 145). In the startling sex scene of chapter 19, Esther's loss of virginity is followed by a severe haemorrhage. Symbolically, this is one of the turning points in Esther's recovery and might be read as a ritualised purgation or blood letting. Only by purging her body can Esther be made whole, or 'fixed' in the words of the emergency room doctor who treats her. The phrase anticipates Esther's description of the rebirth which awaits her at the end of the novel: 'patched, retreaded and approved for the road' (*BJ* 257). In a little-known essay on the book, Hughes proposes that

> The main movement of the action is the shift of the heroine, the 'I', from artificial ego to authentic self – through a painful death . . . The authentic self emerges into fierce rebellion against everything associated with the old ego. Her decisive act (the 'positive' replay of her 'negative' suicide) takes the form of a sanguinary defloration, carefully stage-managed by the heroine, which liberates her authentic self into independence.[32]

In some very early notes on the idea of the novel, Plath muses that 'electrocution [is] brought in . . . waking to a new world, with no name, being born again, and not of woman'.[33]

Images of defilement such as these signify Esther's continuing defiance of the orthodoxies of 1950s America. Lynn Spigel has argued that the 'antiseptic model of space was the reigning aesthetic at the heart of the postwar suburbs'.[34] Esther's unabashed 'puking' and bleeding, her unashamedly dirty hair and her refusal to act with decorum, all signify her resistance. Her rejection of married life with Buddy Willard, or a relationship with Constantin (the substitute proposed by Mrs Willard in his place) mark her out as a refusenik, as a rebel on the same continuum as Esther Ethel Greenglass Rosenberg.

Johnny Panic and the Bible of Dreams

Plath's prose essay 'A Comparison' opens with the exclamation, 'How I envy the novelist!' (*JP* 56). It proceeds to list all the qualities of fiction writing – its capacity to incorporate the random and the quotidian, its inclusiveness, its freedom to move backwards and forwards in time and to shift perspectives (she admires the way in which it 'double exposes' itself, thereby providing a useful metaphor for the duplicitous narrative voice of *The Bell Jar*). Her paean to the novel brings to mind some of Woolf's critical writings. The voice of this brief sketch – knowing, ironic, intimate and provocative in turn – mimics the voice of Woolf's *A Room of One's Own* (1929). It knows itself to be treading on dangerous ground in setting up a distinction, a rivalry even, between poetry and prose. And Plath's uncertainty about which genre she favours is matched by the terms of her own debate (*JP* 57). She sets herself the task of distinguishing between the two genres, but ends up conceding the fluidity of generic boundaries and the futility of attempting to impose any kind of meaningful hierarchy. In refusing to come down definitively on either side of contemporary debates about genre and cultural value, Plath keeps her options open. Her own prose fiction, both *The Bell Jar* and *Johnny Panic*, continues her engagement with these debates.

The stories and sketches now collected as *Johnny Panic and the Bible of Dreams* were assembled in two successive and rather different editions by Hughes. The collection was first published in the UK by Faber and Faber in 1977; a revised edition with an additional nine stories followed two years later. The first US edition, published by Harper & Row in 1979, differed slightly again with the removal of 'A Day in June' and 'The Green Rock' and the inclusion of 'The Smiths: George, Marjorie (5), Claire (16) (Notebooks)'. It also includes a fuller introduction by Hughes than the English editions (*Bib* 49–50). Hughes's introduction to the second English edition explains the background to the selection of stories. The first edition included 'a selection' from some seventeen stories that Plath had assembled at the time of her death. More stories came to light thereafter with the sale of some of Plath's papers to the Lilly Library at Indiana University by her mother (an archive which includes 'typescripts of over fifty stories'). Hughes chose a selection from these mostly early and hitherto unpublished stories for the second edition – stories which he says Plath had already 'failed to publish' and 'rejected' (*JP* 12). *Johnny Panic* also includes fragments and sketches from Plath's *Journals* which were not, at that time, available in the unabridged form subsequently (2000) prepared by Karen V. Kukil. Thus in its revised form (the second UK edition) *Johnny Panic* comprises work ranging across the whole of Plath's writing life and spanning her time in England and the USA.

Value

In his introduction Hughes notes the varying quality of these prose pieces. The structure of the book wherein part one collected the 'more successful' pieces, part two the others, and parts three and four miscellaneous sketches and Lilly archive stories reflects this concern. As Rose has noted, decisions about how to categorise each individual story seem to have been made on grounds other than those relating to publishing success. A previously unpublished story such as 'Snow Blitz', for example, earns its place in part one whereas several previously published stories are relegated to part two.[35] The stories which do earn a place in the 'more successful' category tend to be those which had previously been published in up-market magazines (these include 'The Day Mr Prescott Died', 'The Wishing Box' and 'The Fifteen Dollar Eagle'), while stories which had first appeared in young women's magazines ('Initiation' in *Seventeen* or the prizewinning 'Sunday at the Mintons' in *Mademoiselle*) are moved to part two. The selection criteria, then, seem to exemplify the division between high and low, elite and mass audiences discussed earlier in relation to *The Bell Jar*. Stories written for the literary magazines are met with editorial approval; those written for a female market are marginalised. This is not necessarily a helpful way of categorising Plath's writing. As her *Journals* (and, indeed, 'A Comparison') show, she took each of these markets seriously, researched it carefully and tailored and targeted her work accordingly. The persistent tendency to polarise Plath's work in this way indicates the strength of the challenge she faced as she tried to work across and between distinct genres. Hughes implies in the closing lines of his introduction to *Johnny Panic* that there is more than one writer at work here: 'This collection does not represent the prose of the poet of *Ariel*, any more than the poems of *The Colossus* represent the poetry of the poet of *Ariel*.' It might be more helpful, instead of thinking of Plath's writing as the work of two distinct personae, to consider the way in which she seeks to find a single voice which can encompass multiple subjectivities, and range across disparate forms.

The tension between popular and elite culture, audience and aesthetics, is not mere background to Plath's prose. Rather, it is part and parcel of her subject matter. As Rose argues, 'The problem and divisions of culture are a reiterated theme of her prose writing, the point at which her work turns on itself, making the terms of its cultural production into an object of its own representation.'[36] Nowhere is this clearer than in the early story 'Sunday at the Mintons' (winner of the 1952 *Mademoiselle* short story competition). Here, as Rose goes on to suggest, the collision between elite (masculine) modes of thought and subordinate (female) modes is allegorised in the relationship between Elizabeth Minton and her brother Henry. The focalisation is from Elizabeth's perspective. We see her first 'sigh[ing]' over her brother's fastidiousness, then leaning 'dreamily' across his desk, as though obliterating the masculine order of his work with her prone body (*JP* 148). Plath's point, though subtle, is absolutely fundamental to the story's denouement. The adjectives which dominate the second paragraph of the story equally subtly invite the reader to share the seductiveness of Elizabeth's subsequently much-derided point of view. Through her we notice and enjoy the 'pale squares', 'luminous air' and 'flat sheen of the green ocean'

(*JP* 148). The story proceeds to develop, even to exaggerate, the schism between pleasure (Elizabeth) and purpose (Henry). Henry's role in the family is to monitor Elizabeth's pleasure, to turn it always to purpose or account (*JP* 149). She has developed subtle ways of defying her brother's strictures; she observes him quizzically, quietly mocking his fascination with maps, constellations and calculations (*JP* 154), and she reserves an imaginative and emotional space of her own, imperceptible to her brother and all the more valuable for that.

Axelrod, among others, has spoken of Plath's debt to Woolf, and it is plausible to see shades of *To the Lighthouse* (1927) here when Elizabeth steps free of the house and down to the ocean where she finds her epiphany. Having apparently lost Henry to Neptune's undersea world, she ascends in the opposite direction – taking off like Mary Poppins into the sky above. The scene brings to mind Esther's attempt to escape her past identity by throwing her new clothes to the wind in *The Bell Jar*. In both cases, though, the attempt is foiled. In *The Bell Jar* the oppressive New York heat refuses to carry the clothes away, while the flight of fantasy at the end of 'Sunday at the Mintons' proves to be just that – a figment of Elizabeth's imagination. The closing lines of the story which see Elizabeth reclaimed by her domineering brother are as disappointing for the reader as for Elizabeth herself (*JP* 159). Intriguingly, as Rose shows, an early draft of this story did end with Elizabeth's fully realised transcendence; the final twist was added only shortly before publication.[37]

At the time of its acceptance, Plath was to look on 'Sunday at the Mintons' as a real achievement. Subsequently, however, she was to return to it repeatedly as a symbol of disappointment and failed potential. On 12 July 1958 she despairs that she has been 'spoiled, so spoiled by my early success' (*J* 405). As the next chapter will explain, such fierce self-criticism is wholly characteristic of the *Journals* and notebooks. On 31 May 1959 Plath enjoys a rare reprieve from the constant, self-imposed, pressure to succeed. She has written 'six stories' recently, she explains, the best three in the previous fortnight. Her success, she indicates, is a measure of her perseverance in fighting the 'panic bird' and facing up to 'a blank page day after day' (*J* 486). It is a success, then, which is hard won but nevertheless sets in train a sequence of new ideas, plots and characters (*J* 487–91). For the rest of that month and throughout June, Plath toys with ideas for stories, some of which come to fruition only much later and sometimes in a different form (there is an allusion to a Lazarus theme here, for example, which reemerges in the 1962 poem 'Lady Lazarus') (*J* 497). Plath's sense of a breakthrough at this time anticipates those which were to come later that year in poem after poem during her productive weeks at Yaddo.

The stories Plath celebrates are 'Johnny Panic and the Bible of Dreams', 'The Fifteen Dollar Eagle', 'The Shadow', 'Sweetie Pie and the Gutter Men', 'Above the

Oxbow' and 'This Earth our Hospital' (subsequently retitled 'The Daughters of Blossom Street'). Turning to the title story first, its roots lie in Plath's experience as a part-time secretary in the psychiatric ward of a local hospital during late 1958. It uses the same direct, sardonic, tough voice as is later found in *The Bell Jar* and is all the more unsettling for that. The first person speaker, in what begins like a realistic narrative, explains her role as 'Assistant to the secretary in one of the Out-Patient Departments of the Clinics' Building of the City Hospital' (*JP* 17). This bureaucratic mouthful rapidly gives way to an even more out-landish scene. For the speaker's real 'vocation' is to record other people's dreams. She is at pains to point out that her role is not to control or interpret or judge these dreams; she is the mere passive recipient – a kind of blank page on which other people's fantasies and anxieties might be inscribed. The dream work, to invoke Sigmund Freud's *The Interpretation of Dreams* (1900), proves to be a hard task. Indeed, the speaker seems to have made a form of pact with the devil – a pact which culminates in her ritualised punishment. 'Johnny Panic' subtly leads us from a situation where the speaker is the collector and arbiter of dreams to one where we are all – subject and reader alike – immersed in a nightmare.

Another story from May 1959, 'The Daughters of Blossom Street' (originally 'This Earth Our Hospital'), draws on similar resources. The setting, like that of 'Johnny Panic', is the administration department of a hospital, and the first person protagonist a young woman employed there to keep records. Rather as in the oppressive opening of *The Bell Jar*, pathetic fallacy sets the mood for the narrative to follow. Also as in *The Bell Jar*, the story sets up a complex layering of narratives. In an unusually approving note in her *Journals*, Plath comments on the richness of the story's texture (*J* 527, 496). The grotesqueries of 'The Daughters of Blossom Street' – the various misfits and malcontents it shows – bring to mind the work of the American writer Flannery O'Connor. In both writers' work characters are given space in which to expose themselves and their ideals; in so doing, a mirror is held up to some of the foibles of contemporary society. The multiple layers in 'The Daughters' include the experience of the young female speaker on this storm-ridden evening, the ostensible plot (the illness and death of first one and then another member of staff, Miss Emily and Billy Monihan) and, most importantly, the exploration of the uneasy bonds between women as shaped by the hierarchies of the office. The voice moves from the familiar and colloquial to the sardonic and critical. Mocking the other women's feelings on the death of Billy, she comments, ' "You'd think he'd laid down and died for the whole bunch of us sitting there on those cots" ' (*JP* 91). 'The Fifteen-Dollar Eagle' similarly uses a wisecracking New York idiom which Plath labelled 'first person, slangy' (*J* 509). The rather earlier story 'The Day

Mr Prescott Died' (1956) uses dialogue in a similar way in order to reveal the vanities and deceptions practised by civilised society (*JP* 44–5).

Another earlier story, written in 1956 and thus partway between 'Sunday at the Mintons' of 1952, 'Johnny Panic' and others in the May 1959 group, is 'The Wishing Box'. This, too, explores the relationship between the life of the imagination and reality. This time the gender associations we have noted in the other stories (rational masculinity *vs.* sentimental femininity) are subverted. The effect is subtle but nonetheless compelling. The opening lines associate the habits and tone of voice conventionally attached to one gender with those of the other. Thus Agnes displays the kind of critical certainty typically ascribed to men like Henry Minton whereas her husband, Harold, adopts the passive position more often ascribed to women (he speaks only when spoken to and is vague and 'absent-minded'). Again, the boundaries between the real and the imagined become blurred – dangerously so. Harold's dreams become as important to him as real life: he retells his dreams as though they referred to 'some significant, actual event' (*JP* 49). Agnes's failure to dream, or more properly, as the story qualifies, her failure to generate pleasant dreams that she can recall and retell, becomes even more important than her actual experience. Her hazy and infrequent nightmares refuse interpretation, telling her only that she is inadequate and uninteresting. She succumbs to the unrelenting horrors of her daily experience, unable to ameliorate or escape them through dreams. Her suicide seems, like the ECT treatment of the narrator of 'Johnny Panic', to be some awful form of punishment for not dreaming well enough.

'The Fifty-Ninth Bear' (September 1959) also takes the taut relationship between wife and husband as one of its concerns. In her *Journal* Plath comments with frustration on her inability to plumb the depths of the story. She expresses 'disgust' at the recently completed draft and complains, 'None of the deep emotional undercurrents gone into or developed' (*J* 501). This highly charged narrative opens with the establishment of a rather sinister scene. The contorted and diminished reflection of the setting sun, now as 'red as a dwarf tomato', and the 'sulphurous air' construct a sinister backdrop to the violence which follows. The viewpoint shifts, first from Sadie and Norton together, rather ominously observing a 'ritual of penance and forgiveness' (*JP* 94), then to Norton whose buried anger lies within him, even as he sleeps, like a dark secret (*JP* 95). Sadie's point of view is always mediated by Norton; the reader sees her through his eyes. Nevertheless, it is her desires, moods and habits which dominate the narrative. There is a deep irony here in the gap between Norton's sense of himself as 'Olympian' and indestructible (*JP* 98) and the reader's clear understanding that beneath this surface things might be very different. Norton's manipulation of his wife, his patronising attempt to mediate and thus dominate her experience – he refers to her as 'a lamb on a leash' (*JP* 99) – become, finally, grounds for the violent revenge she wreaks.

English stories

The stories discussed thus far originate in American voices and landscapes. Others, such as 'Stone Boy with Dolphin' and 'Mothers', originate from Plath's time in England, as do the 'Excerpts from Notebooks' collected in part three.

'Mothers', like 'The Daughters of Blossom Street', explores the uneasy bonds of suspicion and mistrust between women. The story has sometimes been read as an indictment of the established Church of England. Kendall, for example, proposes that it 'depicts the local church as persecutory'.[38] However, the story is perhaps more complex than this in its establishment of a dialectic between belonging and exclusion. Mrs Nolan, the presumably Irish, twice-divorced publican's wife, is the obvious scapegoat. But Esther, too, is an outsider. It is not the fact of their marginalisation that is interesting, nor the subtle processes by which they come to be excluded, nor even the role of the established church in determining membership of its Mothers' Union. It is the role of other women in receiving or rejecting incomers, and the nature of Esther's and Mrs Nolan's desire – the ambivalence at the heart of their mixed desperation and revulsion – which make this story really striking.

Plath's third person narrator mimics the tone of an anthropologist here, as in other stories and notebook sketches, such as 'Snow Blitz', discussed below. Her descriptions are careful and evocative, situating these women novitiates in a particular time and place and in a long and worthy tradition – a tradition whose subtleties Esther herself does not yet fully understand, hence her surprise at Mrs Nolan's marginalisation after six years in the area (*JP* 108). Although 'Mothers' gives grounds for mocking the petty snobberies and conventions of church life, there are moments which reveal Esther's profound need for some kind of spiritual bond. Tears prick her eyes when the vicar asks her if she believes in the power of prayer (*JP* 110), the vicar's wife is 'angular, kind' (*JP* 111) and the baby in Esther's womb kicks in what she interprets as a sign of belonging. Disconcerted though she is by the ritual of the service and the tea and the speeches, Esther's story exposes not so much the pettiness of the church or of the Mothers' Union but her own veiled complicity in the exclusionary practices. Her initiation into this world comes with her apparent betrayal, or sacrifice, of Mrs Nolan at the end of the story. Mrs Nolan, Rose and Esther leave the meeting at the same time; Mrs Nolan then goes her own way home while Esther protests to Rose her surprise that the church will not tolerate divorcees.

She then allows Rose to change the subject and, linking arms, affirms her bond with her to the implicit exclusion of Mrs Nolan.

The earlier story 'Initiation' (1952) traces similar themes in an American context at an earlier point in a woman's life; here, in a similarly ambivalent narrative, the heroine, Millicent, first goes along with and then rejects the strictures of the initiation ceremony required to join a college sorority. Yet her final declaration of independence shows her still wanting to appear to play the game, and valuing the eventual prize – of friendship and belonging (*JP* 146). Other sketches of English village life which bear comparison with 'Mothers' include 'Rose and Percy B' and 'Charlie Pollard and the Beekeepers'. These narratives, and contemporaneous notes included as appendices in Plath's *Journals*, indicate that Plath drew on local encounters and experiences for her writing (*JP* 230, 244).

The 1963 sketch 'Snow Blitz' deploys the anthropological or journalistic eye familiar from 'Mothers' in its portrayal of the deprivations of life for a lone American in snowbound London. The story attempts an energetic or sardonic tone; the speaker mocks her own naïvety in thinking that England might have even basic resources for dealing with heavy snow. In so doing, she subtly invites us to share her shock, outrage and disappointment at her powerlessness in these circumstances. As the various petty and not so petty tribulations mount up, we, too, begin to feel overwhelmed. As readers, we grasp at the little moments of cheer in the now unrelenting gloom. The ostensibly upbeat ending which sees the speaker looking to the future and claiming the experience as fine training for her children is undermined by the qualifying 'if' of the final sentence (*JP* 133).

America

'America! America!' (1963) and the fine 'Ocean 1212-W' (1962) turn that same anthropological, defamiliarising eye – now in exile in England – back on the America of Plath's birth. Both pieces are all the more compelling for the distance they encode – a distance which in both cases generates a sense of melancholic loss.

'America! America!' was commissioned by the quintessentially English *Punch* magazine. Plath looks back on her childhood experience during the 1930s and 1940s, invoking stereotypical views of 'melting pot' America, of technological superiority and of national pride (*JP* 34). This celebration of American exceptionalism soon gives way to something rather more searching – both in tone and content. America, it seems, is a harsh place where children's knees are scoured by salty ocean and gritty earth alike, where evil and suspicion lurk unseen.

Plath goes on to expose the terrible double bind, particularly for women of her generation, whereby hard work can bring success but to work too hard and be too successful is seen as unfeminine. The point recalls 'Initiation', 'Mothers' and *The Bell Jar*. In 'America! America!' the speaker looks back on initiation rites and tries to explain her sense of unease with what they required and offered: 'what did these picked buds of American womanhood do at their sorority meetings? They ate cake' (*JP* 37). The story closes by recognising the difference that distance and time have made to her perspective. Imagining looking through the 'plate-glass' wall of a modern American primary school, the narrator laments the loss of something which she conceives of as somehow more real, more authentic, than the present (*JP* 38).

'Ocean 1212-W' also looks back to the contours of an American childhood. The image of glass in 'America! America!' which exposes the insubstantiality of present-day life emerges in slightly different form in 'Ocean 1212-W' as a medium by which the past is preserved. The ocean offers a 'mirrory pool' and a 'looking glass' wherein the Narcissus-like child finds her identity. Later, the speaker laments not what she can see through the glass (as in 'America! America!') but the fact that what she can see, she can no longer access. Her memories have 'sealed themselves off like a ship in a bottle – beautiful, inaccessible, obsolete, a fine, white flying myth' (*JP* 124). The moment which is most memorable, or more properly, most representative, is the moment when all this was finally lost to the speaker – the 'one day' heralded by the birth of a sibling, when the child no longer experiences a symbiotic union with the world around her and learns, for the first time, separation, isolation and identity: 'I felt the wall of my skin: I am I' (*JP* 120). For Elisabeth Bronfen, the separation from this seascape is 'inextricably linked to the figure of the father . . . because his death was the reason [the speaker's] family moved inland'. In her other writing, according to Bronfen, Plath 'repeatedly invokes the lost father as a metonymy for this lost scene of childhood bliss, with both standing in for the state of happiness whose value resides precisely in its irrecuperability'.[39] From this point of view, the memories are not sealed off because they are precious, they are precious because they are irrevocably sealed off, lost, out of reach.

It is possible to read both these stories – rather like a number of the poems discussed earlier – as only partly about their ostensible theme of American childhood. They are also, more importantly, about the aesthetic processes by which such memories might be accessed, mediated and shared. Metaphorically, the essays register, exemplify and lament their failure truly to do justice to the past which is always lost to us and no longer accessible – even by the unpredictable magic of words.

Chapter 6

Letters Home and *Journals*

Letters Home

Commentators have called the 1975 publication of *Letters Home*, edited by Aurelia Plath, a 'corrective' or an 'antidote' to *The Bell Jar*.[1] As we have seen, the novel was not originally intended for publication in the USA. Once it became clear that it was necessary legally, and attractive financially so to do, Aurelia was persuaded not to veto its appearance.[2] Nevertheless, she experienced the book as a bitter and ungrateful attack by her daughter on those she knew and loved. Its immediate popularity on its April 1971 appearance in the USA (it spent five months in the bestseller charts) coupled with the by then well-known 'back story' emerging from *Ariel* and other posthumous poems, meant that – as Aurelia had feared – the novel was widely read (even, as Tracy Brain's *The Other Sylvia Plath* points out, promoted) as an autobiographical study.

In her 1983 essay, ironically written in the form of a letter and published in Paul Alexander's 1985 *Ariel Ascending*, Aurelia describes her dismay at the 'violation' she saw in *The Bell Jar*. There, as we saw in Chapter 5, she argues that her daughter's art 'transformed personalities into cruel and false caricatures'. The effect is all the more shocking, it seems, when compared with the 'close, affectionate . . . good, supportive' and 'wholesome' life that the mother had, in her own version of 'actuality', been able to provide.[3] *Letters Home* was conceived as an attempt to put this record straight. Diane Middlebrook explains: 'Public discussion of [*The Bell Jar*] confirmed Aurelia's dread that readers would identify the heroine Esther with Sylvia, and Esther's mother with Aurelia . . . she came up with a plan to recover her reputation: she proposed to Hughes that she edit a book of Plath's letters, which Aurelia hoped would counteract these negative images.'[4] Just as Aurelia had been reluctant to sanction the US publication of *The Bell Jar*, Ted Hughes was less than enthusiastic about the plan to publish a selection from Plath's letters. According to Marjorie Perloff, he requested the excision of certain letters and details from what was, at first, a 1,000 page, two-volume draft.[5] Perloff quotes *The New York Times Book Review*'s assertion that:

> A lot of Mr. Hughes's deletions had to do with protecting the privacy of the couple's two children, removing private domestic details and excising some tart references by Miss Plath to contemporaries; he also removed some glowing descriptions of himself in early love letters. At this point, Harper and Row's lawyers took charge, simply restoring those that presented no libel or invasion of privacy problems and discarding those that possibly did.

At stake for Ted Hughes and for Aurelia Plath are issues of privacy and truth; the task for them both is to reconcile commercial, legal, aesthetic and personal demands with their sense of responsibility – to the work, to the children, to friends, family, Plath's memory and themselves. Debates about ethics, value and interpretation, which began with the posthumous publication of key poems and continued with the appearance in the USA of *The Bell Jar* and the emergence of various personal memoirs (including Al Alvarez's *The Savage God* and Nancy Hunter Steiner's 1973 *A Closer Look at Ariel*), are crystallised in the publishing history of *Letters Home* and carry over into the *Journals*, into Hughes's *Birthday Letters* (1998) and beyond. *Letters Home* provokes questions about the relationship between private experience and its public representation, and between truth and its revelation. What kind of responsibility does the speaker bear to her own experience, to the experience of other parties, and to her readers? What difference does it make to the reader that they are reading letters which although not explicitly addressed to them, implicitly invite their attention and response? As with Robert Lowell's 1973 collection *The Dolphin* (which appropriates letters from his estranged wife) and Hughes's *Birthday Letters*, the trope of the letter forces a confrontation – on the part of poet and reader alike – with issues of privacy, revelation, honesty, subjectivity, audience and response.

It is evident from the range of Plath's writing discussed thus far that she uses different genres, modes and forms in order to find, manipulate, disguise, confront or display many different versions of the 'I'. The effect is seen particularly acutely in the form of the letter, the conventions of which permit the construction of an epistolary 'I' who apostrophises a real or imagined 'you'. The 'I' may well be authentic and self-disclosing, but it may also be a form of evasion or pretence. Janet Altman characterises letter writing as 'truly a communication with spectres, not only with the spectre of the addressee but also with one's own phantom, which evolves underneath one's own hand in the very letter one is writing'.[6] Thus the 'I' is constructed in the process of writing the letters and is produced by, rather than reflected in, the epistolary exchange. The same might also be said of the broader genre of life writing. In the case of *Letters Home*, the speaker from the outset is engaged in the process of finding and/or displaying a specific form of identity – one which is shaped by the discursive relationship with the primary addressee.

The selection of letters that Aurelia finally arrived at was published in the USA by Harper & Row in 1975 and in the UK by Faber and Faber the following year. Comprising some 700 letters, *Letters Home* spans Plath's years at Smith College during the early 1950s, her time in Cambridge and Devon, and the final months in London in late 1962 and early 1963. The collection develops a narrative structure – the structure of a novel that Hughes urged Aurelia to impose (*LTH* 352). However, if what Hughes meant by this suggestion was that the book should be understood as a form of fictionalisation – as creative, constructed, mediated – the opposite was to happen. One early reviewer notes that the 'cumulative effect is that of an autobiography'.[7]

Other critics, too, have looked to the letters for evidence of the life of the author. Erica Jong praises the collection for the 'understanding of Plath' which the letters provide.[8] Plath's letters are not alone in being received in this way. The editor of Elizabeth Bishop's letters, *One Art* (1994), for example, suggests that they 'in a sense . . . constitute her autobiography'. However, as he goes on to say, 'They were not intended as such: she was *not* recording her life but was simply keeping in touch with her friends and correspondents.'[9] In the letters of Plath's contemporaries, it is often exchanges between writers, or between writers and editors, even between writers and enthusiastic fans, that provide the richest insights into a poet's writing practices. *Letters Home* is, of course, quite different from this; the book does not present the selected correspondence of one writer with a range of others. Instead, it offers the inevitably narrow – indeed one-sided – correspondence between one person and another. Although Aurelia reproduces a small number of letters between Plath and her brother Warren and mentor Olive Higgins Prouty, these represent a small proportion of the whole. As the collected letters of other poets of Plath's generation (Bishop, Marianne Moore, Robert Lowell and Anne Sexton) show, and the archival research of scholars such as Tracy Brain attest, a wider selection of Plath's correspondence might provide a quite different picture and would be a rich and rewarding resource.

From the moment of first publication, the question of the value of these letters to an appreciation of Plath's creative processes has been an important one. Jong, in the review quoted above, suggests that these letters help us the better to understand the work. Anne Tyler, on the other hand, argues that they do not offer any great insight: 'The letters are not going to be much help to scholars, and in content they are not very unusual.' Carol Bere compromises with the assertion that the letters, though generally limited in value, tell us much about the 'early work'.[10] At first sight, Bere's seems like a promising rationale and strategy for reading *Letters Home*. If the correspondence can offer clues about the writing process, we may better understand and appreciate the poems. I will tentatively suggest some fruitful links between letters and particular poems, voices or aesthetic practices shortly. However, we would be wise to register as well the limitations of attempting such an approach. Firstly, it might be useful to consider these letters not simply as background evidence, valuable only for what they tell us about our true object of concern (implicitly, the *Ariel* poems), but as excursions into a new genre, and thus valuable in their own right. Secondly, even if we do choose to read these letters as providing a key to the poems, we need to recognise the limitations and partiality of the evidence they provide. Furthermore, to read the letters as supplying insights into how the poems work, or in order to decipher their 'true' meaning, is to set up a hierarchy of texts and of textual authority which Plath herself might have been loth to concede. As her short fiction shows, she sought success in a range of different forms, and developed voices and strategies to enable her to achieve it. Finally, if we recognise that Plath is exercised by the fluidity and noncoherence of language and the multiplicity of subjectivity, it will prove hard to justify using these letters as a form of evidence for what the 'real' Plath really meant.

Reading *Letters Home* for an insight into Plath's writing practice is, then, a potentially problematic approach. Nevertheless, many of these letters reveal something about Plath's careful scrutiny of the editorial preferences and target audiences of her chosen journals and magazines (*LH* 107, 230, 290, 301, 312, 401, 403). There are also allusions to the diligence and discipline she sees as necessary to her success (*LH* 92, 105, 148) and to Hughes's role in introducing new influences and new vocabulary, and providing writing tasks and exercises to develop her skills as a writer (*LH* 235, 267). They provide insight into the sources of some of the poems (of 'Wuthering Heights', for example (*LH* 268), and 'The Operation' (*LH* 412)) and into the gradual emergence of *The Colossus* in 1960 (*LH* 281, 287, 343, 366, 417) and of a number of the stories (*LH* 84, 87, 155, 262–5, 349). They also disclose Plath's much-cited comments about the *Ariel* poems which, in a letter of 12 October 1962, she describes as 'terrific stuff' and, four days later, as 'the best poems of my life' (*LH* 466, 468).

Finally, these letters work not just as an account of lived experience, or of the practices of a writer, or as an aesthetic form in their own right, but as a narrative of a social and cultural context (what Jong calls 'the story of what it means to be a woman of genius in a world in which most of the nurturing is reserved for men of genius') and a 'view of a system of values'.[11] They cover – albeit sometimes implicitly or in passing – many of the key historical and political figures and concerns of mid-century American and British life: the Suez crisis (*LH* 282, 284), President Dwight D. Eisenhower (*LH* 96, 149), the Aldermaston march and nascent Campaign for Nuclear Disarmament (*LH* 378), the military/industrial complex (*LH* 437) and consumerism (*LH* 342).

Rendering account

The earliest of the *Letters Home* are written by Plath when she has newly arrived, as a seventeen-year-old student, at Smith College. She is working hard to find herself in a culture which defines young women by their peer popularity, academic ability and demonstrable success with boys. A letter of 30 September 1950 shows her consciously assembling pieces of her adult identity – an identity which only begins to fall into place when she lands her first 'college date' (*LH* 48). Subsequently, we see her trying to calibrate and recalibrate her position among fellow students (first at Smith and later at Cambridge), other poets (male and female, English and American), fellow professors, mentors, family, husband and, finally, children. She refers several times to the difficulties of reconciling apparently contradictory roles, or divergent 'I's (*LH* 219, 239) but she also recognises that she cannot assume one 'I' alone: 'I have to begin life on *all* fronts', as she urges herself (and reassures her mother) on arrival in Cambridge in 1955 (*LH* 185).

These letters emerge from a highly pressured and intense atmosphere. This is partly culturally inscribed, partly self-inflicted and partly generated by the complexities of the relationship between the speaker and her self-sacrificing and aspirational mother. Perloff argues that these letters – like the poems – are written with a fierce determination 'to please and impress her mother' and the various others whose esteem she counted on. She further notes that it is after her mother has witnessed in person the breakdown of her marriage to Hughes, and thus the crack in the carefully contrived mask presented in the letters, that Plath drops the cheery moniker 'Sivvy' with which she had hitherto signed off the letters, and reverts to plain 'Sylvia'.[12] The Plath we see throughout these letters is, then, constantly striving to live up to her own and others' expectations (*LH* 56, 57). The early letters veer from a sense of urgency (*LH* 53, 67) to one of lassitude (*LH* 83). The difference within and between letters is striking. There is a fine line, it seems, between moments of ambition and optimism and utter abjection. The writer seems acutely aware of, even guilty about, the effect that some of her less optimistic letters will have on her reader, attempting to reassert balance, as the 1955 letter quoted above indicates, by making the next more positive in tone (compare, for example, the letters of 3 and 5 October 1955 or the very different letters of 24 and 25 February 1956).

From the Smith years onwards, defining and contradictory tropes emerge. These include a tendency to 'protest too much' about how greatly she is enjoying everything, coupled with repeated attempts to head off her (and arguably her mother's) worst fears by anticipating and embracing them. The two moods are brought into self-paralysing conflict on occasions when moments of apparent delight and success are modified or qualified by the desire for more, or anticipation of the next achievement, or anxiety about this particular moment turning to failure (*LH* 109, 113, 123, 248). Repeatedly, Plath's letters prepare herself, and crucially her mother, for as yet unconfirmed disappointments, slights and hurts. In this way, she defuses, diverts or assimilates the painful knocks she dreads receiving. In a letter of 31 October 1950, for example, Plath reports back to her mother on a routine interview with Smith College's Director of Scholarships. She comments first on how happy she is, and then concedes her desperate hope that she may live up to the expectations placed on her (*LH* 56). In March 1953 successive letters recount a series of setbacks from which Plath attempts to rise by counting her blessings (*LH* 106–7). Later in her career, in a letter of 19 November 1960, Plath writes to her mother of the imminent publication of the UK edition of *The Colossus* but is at pains to dampen her mother's (and perhaps also her own) expectations: 'it's a nice gift book', she demurs, before pointing out how little money she expects to make (*LH* 399–400).

My assertion that Plath 'reports back' to Aurelia is no mere turn of phrase. These letters represent Plath's dutiful rendering of account to her mother; they provide a means of formally acknowledging and reconciling Aurelia's emotional and financial investment in the daughter, and of seeking her ongoing approval. Repeatedly in *Letters Home*, Plath tries to turn adversity to account. She tolerates a dreadful summer job on the grounds that she will be recompensed by good material for stories (*LH* 89). The examples of Plath's mother and of her mentor, Olive Higgins Prouty, are arguably instrumental in instilling this attitude. In a letter to Aurelia of 2 September 1953, Higgins Prouty highlights the redeeming lessons of her own mental breakdown some twenty-five years earlier (*LH* 127). Plath learns to read difficulties in her life as challenges which will turn her into a better person (*LH* 215, 244), or at least she learns that by presenting problems in this way – as adversities to be determinedly overcome – she can share them with her mother. Despair, it seems, will not be tolerated in that quarter. Despair tempered with a cheerful resolve to outwit it, just might.

The rhetoric of cancelling out and of imposing checks and balances is fundamental to *Letters Home*. Christina Britzolakis describes the collection as 'an accounting to Aurelia – lists of prizes and awards with their monetary value reckoned and invoiced'.[13] Plath's sense of her debt to her mother is explicit throughout the book from the moment in June 1952 when she receives news of her $500 prize in the *Mademoiselle* competition, which she immediately converts in her mind into a material reward for her mother ('pretty clothes or a special trip' (*LH* 86)) to a letter of May 1955 about another happy success. This news is accompanied by a statement of account in which Plath renders the prize money won that year and implicitly owed to the mother (*LH* 175–6). On 28 February 1953 she writes of her hope that one day she will be able to pay her mother back for her hard work and the sacrifices she seems to have made in order to ensure her children's success. Her birthday present to her mother in April 1953 is cabled news of acceptances and prizes totalling $110 (*LH* 109). To her brother, Warren, in May of that year, she says of her mother that they should both start repaying her with 'dividends of joy' (*LH* 113). To Aurelia, in the same month, she insists, '[y]ou deserve all the returns' (*LH* 114). This rendering of monies owed takes on uncomfortable tones in an unsent letter dated 28 February 1953 in which Plath looks back on her suicide attempt earlier that year, rationalising it as 'more merciful and inexpensive' than the alternative – a lifetime of mental illness and costly long-term treatment (*LH* 130).

As important as the accounting to the mother, though, is the accounting to and of the self. In his essay 'Technologies of the Self' (1988), the philosopher Michel Foucault traces the changing rituals or 'technologies of the self' from the ancient Greek admonition to take care of oneself to the more modern imperative to know oneself and to reveal oneself to God or other authority figures (arguably, in Plath's case, to her mother). To know oneself, in this context, requires a careful keeping and rendering of account or a form of 'vigilance'. In the present era techniques of verbalisation are used 'without renunciation of the self . . . to constitute, positively, a new self'.[14] Thus *Letters Home* represents a way for Plath of accounting to herself (and to her mother) for her actions, subjecting them to rigorous scrutiny – both her own and that of her addressee – and thereby shaping a form of subjectivity. Letters of 30 August and 13 October 1954 see Plath carefully and consciously articulating her position, her identity; she strives to know herself in order to gain the approval, assent or forgiveness of her mother.

Leaving home

In terms of the narrative structure of *Letters Home*, there is a clear change in tone and content as the book proceeds, with the later letters more interested in reporting events, experiences and opportunities than in communicating setbacks or demonstrating admirable responses to obstacles that have been set in the speaker's way. From late 1962 onwards, after the breakdown of her marriage, Plath's letters are preoccupied with arrangements. Her strategy for coping with her current circumstances is to lay complex plans that at least promise a way out (*LH* 461, 465, 469). Even here, though, we see Plath regressing (interestingly, this is a word she uses of her daughter Frieda's response to the breakdown of her parents' marriage) to the alternating pattern of letters of despair succeeded by letters of hope, which we noted earlier (*LH* 464, 466).

Most importantly, we begin to see Plath's separation from the mother who, for the critic Rose Kamel, figures as an 'anti-self' – someone who Plath 'feared, yet deeply loved and identified with'. In Steven Gould Axelrod's words, the two exist in a 'tension-filled hypersymbiosis'.[15] In *The Bell Jar*, the moment when Esther recognises and can utter her hatred for her mother is the moment when she turns her back on sickness and towards health. As early as 1960 – that is, after Plath has become a mother herself – she begins forcibly to reject her mother's advice, for example about growth hormones (*LH* 376). A month later, she insists twice that her mother desist from directing enquiring readers to her address (*LH* 384). Plath's attempt to establish some boundaries brings to mind the fear of the penetration of those boundaries expressed in 'Medusa'. In the late letters in particular, we see the same pattern. As is well documented in numerous biographies, Aurelia was staying with her daughter in Devon in the summer of 1962 at around the time when the marriage began to fail. Plath, it seems, was traumatised by her mother's witnessing of these events. In a letter of 9 October 1962, she insists that in the light of this, she does not wish to see her mother again. Moreover, she forcefully rejects her platitudes, her sentimentality and her habit of showing, and expecting, fortitude in adversity. In a frequently cited letter dated 25 October 1962, Plath angrily tells her mother to stop trying to fortify her by referring her to sentimental stories in the *Ladies' Home Journal* and to accept the ugly, grotesque reality of life (which clearly is not the same as Aurelia's 'actuality') in its place. For Perloff, Plath's turn away from the sentimental, idealised worldview promoted by women's magazines, after years of trying to assimilate their style and to gain recognition and recompense from those quarters, is a final rejection of the mother's aspirations for her daughter. Quoting the letter cited above, Perloff concludes, 'Here Sivvy has finally given way to Sylvia.'[16]

The Journals of Sylvia Plath

The circumstances surrounding the publication of Plath's *Journals* are, as one might expect, as contentious as those surrounding her other posthumous writings. If anything, the situation with the *Journals* is more problematic, given that these are ostensibly private writings which one must assume, given the absence of evidence to the contrary, were never meant for public consumption.[17] Hughes was later to refer to the 'explosive drama' surrounding the process of preparing the book for publication, ruefully noting that this was 'only the beginning of bigger explosions'.[18] Decisions about when, how and why to publish this disparate mass of material are, not surprisingly, fraught with complications. Moreover, as Brain notes, there is little certainty about what, exactly, is meant by Plath's *Journals*. What have been described and collected as 'journals' in fact comprise all manner of items including

> [h]andwriting in store-bought bound and spiral notebooks, typing on
> miscellaneous pieces of paper, and scrawls on sheets of varying degrees
> of size, colour, type and formality . . . while the 'journals' are officially
> lodged in Smith College's Rare Book Room, the Lilly Library also
> possesses papers and small calendars in which Plath jotted her thoughts.
> These might also legitimately constitute Plath's 'journals'.[19]

Plath's *Journals* have been published in two entirely different editions, separated by almost twenty years. *The Journals of Sylvia Plath*, edited by Frances McCullough (with Hughes in the role of 'Consulting Editor') and comprising only a fraction of the extant material, appeared in 1982 in the USA only. In 2000 *The Journals of Sylvia Plath: 1950–1962* and *The Unabridged Journals of Sylvia Plath*, both edited by Karen V. Kukil, appeared in the UK and the USA respectively. I will proceed by briefly discussing the earlier, McCullough edition, before turning to the changes and additions in the later complete edition.

The Journals of Sylvia Plath (1982): the abridged edition

As we have seen, Hughes issued an edition of Plath's *Ariel* in 1965 and was, arguably, left with no option but to publish a US edition of *The Bell Jar* some six years later. Partly in response to this, Aurelia published Plath's *Letters Home*. Running in tandem with these 'authorised' editions of Plath's writing were new biographical and critical interpretations of her life and work. According to Middlebrook, it was the combination of Hughes's careful work in the archive as he checked the early drafts of *Letters Home* and his alarm at what he perceived to be the speculations and misinterpretations of others that galvanised him into preparing an edition of the *Journals*. Into this mix, as always (and this, incidentally, is a recurrent theme of Plath's writing in the *Journals* as in *Letters Home*) comes money and the question of the financial returns which might accrue from such a project. Middlebrook reports that Hughes was at this time faced with a significant tax bill; the royalties from the bestselling 1971 edition of *The Bell Jar* had, apparently, been inadequately accounted for by Hughes's advisers. To make up the shortfall, Hughes arranged the sale of Plath's archive to Smith College and agreed, albeit equivocally, to the publication of an abridged edition of her personal writings.[20]

This 1982 edition of the *Journals* includes, by Hughes's own admission, about 'a third of the whole bulk' (*J Abr.* xv). The selection ranges from the summer of 1950 when Plath took various vacation jobs before enrolling at Smith College, through her years as a Fulbright Scholar at Cambridge University (1955–7) to a few final entries and observations from her time in London and Devon (1960–2). The journals proper, as Hughes points out, close at the end of 1959. The later London and Devon entries selected for the abridged edition are fragments of longer pieces which the later edition includes in full. There are other omissions, including two volumes spanning 1960 to 1963 which Hughes concedes are missing (one presumed lost and one which he 'destroyed . . . because I did not want her children to have to read it' (*J Abr.* xv)). As Middlebrook notes, Hughes's admission that one journal has disappeared, and the other been destroyed, appears here as just an afterthought. Janet Malcolm discusses the various versions of this brief foreword (expanded for publication in the journal *Grand Street* in 1982 and subsequently reprinted in Alexander's *Ariel Ascending* and in Hughes's *Winter Pollen* (1994)), indicating that the order of appearance of this confession, and thus its significance to the essay as a whole, changes over time.[21] There are two further volumes which the foreword to the abridged edition does not mention, but which the later complete version makes clear were originally sealed from view until 2013 (fifty years after Plath's death) (*J* ix) but were opened by Hughes just before his death in 1998.

If the origins of these *Journals* remain cloudy, so, too, Hughes's foreword to the book seems unclear. The foreword to the abridged edition runs to just over two pages and focuses on the relationship between these prose entries and Plath's other work. Hughes suggests that the value of the journal entries lies, paradoxically, both in their separation from the market- or audience-oriented nature of her other writing (which, he says, 'suffered from her ambition' to place it in specific magazines) and in the insights they offer into her fundamental 'impulse' and 'ideals' (*J Abr.* xiii). He uses this foreword to establish what was to become a dominant narrative in Plath studies for many years.

This vision traces a steady, inexorable and wholly necessary – if painful – movement in Plath's work from youthful and superficial polish to mature, triumphant self-realisation. Hughes's foreword establishes the *Journal* entries as background evidence for the struggle between two selves which, he argues, we see in the poetry (*J Abr.* xv). This narrative has had its dissenters of late. Even at the time of writing, though, there were some who demurred from Hughes's account. Miriam Levine, for example, writing in 1983, observes, 'When I read Hughes' introduction to the journals, I was not convinced by his statement of Plath's true birth into herself. I found instead her brilliant mastery, her heroic burning through to describe the landscape of desolation . . . her fall from grace, her incomplete self.'[22] As though in an attempt to head off speculation by Edward Butscher and other early biographers, Hughes insists that 'this is her autobiography'. However, in the same breath he acknowledges that it is 'far from complete' and, more importantly, that even as autobiography, what it captures is not the real life, but the process of 'unmaking and remaking' the self (*J Abr.* xv). Unwittingly, perhaps, Hughes concedes some of the key understandings of some recent readings of Plath's life and work – for example, the supposition that any attempt at self-representation might more usefully be thought of as a process of self-constitution in language. We will return to perspectives such as these in the next chapter. Hughes, then, presents the *Journals* as the background story, valuable primarily because of what they tell us about how she arrived at, and found her true self in, the poems of *Ariel* (*J Abr.* xv).

The longer version of Hughes's foreword, mentioned earlier, is rather different. Hughes speaks in the third instead of the first person and employs a more authoritative, and perhaps defiant, tone than in the shorter version. He is more specific about some of the ethical issues which arise when editing, and by implication reading, material of this kind. If the editor ('her husband', as he refers to himself) is aware of his responsibility in releasing this material into the public domain, he is equally intent on reminding the readers of their responsibility – a responsibility to read correctly (or not to give way to 'evident confusions'). In providing this 'curtailed journal', Hughes – like Aurelia with *Letters Home* – aims to provide 'ballast', or evidence, with which to balance out or correct the dangerous 'hypotheses' inspired by the poems or the 'errant versions' of biography (*WP* 177). As the next chapter will make clear, Hughes is treading difficult ground here. He implies that there is a direct, if as yet misunderstood, relationship between the poetry and the life – a relationship which the publication of these *Journals* will help to clarify. Elsewhere, though, he has fought shy of reading the diaries in this way, concurring with Malcolm's view that they are practice pieces 'shaping up for some possible novel, little chapters for novels . . . She thought of her journals as working notes for some ultimate novel . . . She changed certain things to make them *work* [his emphasis], to make some kind of symbolic statement of a feeling. She wasn't writing an account of this or that event'.[23] Much early criticism of Plath (as indeed of other personal or confessional poets) did assume a direct link between experience and representation. Of late, exciting new work on Plath, particularly that deriving from psychoanalytical and poststructuralist perspectives, but also from other angles including some which attempt a return to the neutral, objective New Criticism so dominant in Plath's own era, has turned its back on such assumptions. These new perspectives insist on the impossibility of knowing or reading such links and on the far more interesting qualities of the poetic text, devoid of any biographical or historical speculations.

Masks

The journal entries offer an insight into what Plath herself called her many masks. There are numerous voices and moods here. Rather as in *Letters Home*, these can change suddenly and devastatingly. The Benidorm entries, for example, shift so utterly as to profoundly unsettle the reader's confidence in the reliability of the voice they deploy (*J Abr.* 144–7). Plath is able here to work through deeply held anxieties and desires, to express her despair, rage and ennui and to find space for her fiercely self-willed optimism. Again as in *Letters Home*, Plath self-consciously constructs a personal identity (*J Abr.* 296, 300, 315, 330). But she is also able to deconstruct that identity and to dissociate the subject and object 'I' (the person speaking and the person spoken about). In this separation (which mimics that in *The Bell Jar*), there is often a profound irony. Moreover, she sometimes shifts into a different register, speaking to herself in the second person as though dispassionately to describe or assess her motives and actions (*J Abr.* 24).

Many of these entries illuminate the sources of key poems, such as 'In Plaster' (*J Abr.* 74). They also reveal Plath's diligent work in selecting the right markets to which to direct material (*J Abr.* 169–70), her fear of creative paralysis (*J Abr.* 155 and 187) and the influence of other writers and artists (*J Abr.* 211, 292–3). The most contentious and personal comments have, as editor Frances McCullough explains, been cut: 'There are quite a few nasty bits missing – Plath had a very sharp tongue and tended to use it on nearly everybody' (*J Abr.* xii). Nevertheless, enough remains to suggest that within the private space of her own notebook, Plath could be critical, hostile and even vicious. An entry of 19 May 1958 records her hostility towards people encountered at a play reading at Smith College: 'a fat girl and ugly man . . . the corrupt, white snail-faced

Van Voris, whose voice, luxuriated over the words: loins, incest, bed, foul' (*J Abr.* 229). Later, her anger spills over into barely controlled fury – a rage whose extremity she later reflects on – at seeing some girls carelessly tearing at the rhododendron flowers in a public park (*J Abr.* 227–36, 255).

Hughes's attempt to find 'ballast' in cases such as these results in he and McCullough inserting additional notes which, though kept to a minimum and usually insightful (*J Abr.* xii), sometimes attempt to steer interpretation or to proffer some kind of apologia. When Plath makes some mildly judgemental comments about her grandmother, the editorial note assures us that the entry is misleading and that she did 'in fact adore her grandmother' (*J Abr.* 24). Later still, edited selections from entries discussing Plath's renewed therapy with Dr Ruth Beuscher are introduced with a warning note from Aurelia. This intervention alone provides ample evidence of the uneasy accommodation and the compromises which must have been negotiated behind the scenes before this book could make it into print (*J Abr.* 265). Brain, glossing Jacqueline Rose, further notes that in the editorial process what has gone missing are 'references to Plath's politics, references to sex, "selective" references to real people, Plath's "experiments with popular fictional forms", and passages where she expresses happiness'.[24] McCullough's declared intention in editing this selection from the journals is to let the material 'speak for itself' (*J Abr.* xii). However, what is most notable here are the gaps, elisions and interpretative barriers which seem, precisely, to prevent that. As an early review in *McLean's Magazine* protests:

> Apart from protecting real people from damaging remarks, there is no need to protect the reader from Plath herself. The decision to publish her journals should respect her contradictory selves; instead, the editing makes us feel that Plath's husband, mother and editor are peering over our shoulders as we read, much in the way Plath hallucinated them peering over hers as she wrote.[25]

The Journals of Sylvia Plath (2000): the unabridged edition

UK and US editions of Plath's unabridged journals, edited by Karen V. Kukil, appeared in 2000. Their publication was celebrated by many as the long-awaited key to Plath's back story. However, Rose sounds a note of caution: it is a 'mistake', she says, 'to see these journals as giving us access to some new or previously hidden "truth"'. They are valuable, instead, 'because evidence can be found within them to support every single theory that has ever been produced about Sylvia Plath'.[26]

As we have seen, McCullough closes her introductory note to her abridged edition by expressing the hope that the book will 'speak for itself'. The opening sentence of Kukil's preface to her edition insists that it does precisely this: 'Sylvia Plath speaks for herself in this unabridged edition of her journals' (*J* ix). Her implicit riposte to the earlier volume gives way to a clear and full description of the material which follows: 'an exact and complete transcription of twenty-three original manuscripts' held in the archive at Smith College. Kukil's volume also includes the two journals, spanning August 1957 to November 1959, which had hitherto been restricted by Hughes until fifty years after Plath's death but had recently been reopened. Kukil is careful to clarify the facsimile-like qualities of her edition; all entries are transcribed exactly without any correction or alteration. The aim throughout has been 'to give the reader direct access to Sylvia Plath's actual words without interruption or interpretation' (*J* x). These editorial principles are slightly different in the US edition, though, where '"twelve sentences" have been omitted . . . and some names have been disguised', apparently to protect individuals from remarks made about their alleged impotence or medical conditions.[27]

The intensity of the near-700 pages of entries encapsulates a range of themes, concerns and voices. The voices vacillate between the twin poles of self-enforced optimism (*J* 296, 486) and, more frequently, self-disgust (*J* 169, 284), depression (*J* 202), despair (*J* 273), self-loathing (*J* 386), fearful paralysis (*J* 404, 522), anger (*J* 395) and jealousy (*J* 480, 485). Plath tacitly recognises the coexistence of these extremes in the rhododendron episode cited earlier. On later examining her mood, Plath notes, '[i]t is as if my life were magically run by two electric currents: joyous positive and despairing negative' (*J* 395).

Rather as in *Letters Home*, the *Journals* provide Plath with the opportunity to scrutinise herself, to identify, castigate and correct her failings. Again, these moments of self-knowledge – or strategies and techniques for developing an understanding of the self – are reminiscent of what Foucault calls 'technologies of the self'. The self that Plath finds or constructs is often found to be at fault and must repeatedly be criticised and punished. The perpetual self-incrimination in these *Journals* rapidly becomes exhausting. The writer and her work seem indivisible; every rejection is experienced as a punishment, and what is worse, one that the speaker deserves. All seems to hang on external confirmation – at first, on social acceptance as signified by a college date (*J* 160), but more and more, as the *Journals* proceed, on acceptance as a writer. The speaker, at times, seems trapped in a cycle of despair with nothing to look forward to except 'a malicious perpetual future' (*J* 176). Failures and potential failures crowd her waking (and dreaming) life such that the moments of success, though they blaze bright, cannot penetrate for long the gloomy memories of earlier despair or the dreadful anticipation of the next fall. As a perceptive entry of 19 July 1958 puts it, 'My worst habit is my fear and my destructive rationalizing' (*J* 408).

The scrutiny is not only internal, though. The self-interrogation and self-surveillance are of the outer surface, too. In an entry of September 1952, Plath castigates herself after an unsuccessful date for not bothering to wear high-heeled shoes (*J* 145). Four months later, on 10 January 1953, she pastes a photograph of herself to the page of the journal and instructs herself to 'look at that ugly dead mask' and 'not forget it' (*J* 155). Entries such as this punctuate the *Journals* and remind us of a number of factors. Firstly, they offer a valuable reminder of the social expectations of young women during this period. The destiny of bright young women of Plath's generation was to fulfil their potential, repay their parents and sponsors, attract and keep a mate, and inculcate their offspring in the way society deemed appropriate. Secondly, they remind us how deeply entwined all these separate identities were for Plath. Success in one field was not enough – and mere adequacy in a number of areas was no substitute. This places Plath in an impossible and deeply frustrating situation: 'I am torn in different directions, pulled thin', she explains during her first term at Smith; 'I can never be all the people I want and live all the lives I want' (*J* 27, 43).

A consequence of this is a kind of paralysis, produced by what Plath recognises as a fear of leaping into situations which might 'close off alternatives' (*J* 445). The point is reminiscent of the metaphor of the fig tree in *The Bell Jar* wherein Esther is unable to choose between any of the symbolic figs dangling in front of her eyes. Betty Friedan was to recognise a similar moment of crisis in *The Feminine Mystique* (1963): 'What if the terror a girl faces at twenty-one is the terror of freedom to decide her own life, with no one to order which path she will take?'[28] For Plath, the sense that the writing life is the scene of paralysis or suffocation recurs again and again in these journals. As early as the summer of 1951, she speaks of feelings of paralysis and numbness. Problems with her vacation job give rise to a sense of oppression and constraint which is played out in the body. She feels, she writes, as though 'all your outlets are blocked, as with wax'. It is significant that Plath shifts into the second person here, addressing herself as though she were another, and thereby gaining a saving distance from, and finding a voice for, her otherwise occluded distress (*J* 84). In November of the following year, exhausted and overwhelmed by a list of tasks to perform, Plath declares herself 'hollow'. Her eyes, she says, mask a 'numb, paralyzed cavern' (*J* 149). The image of the eyes as unseeing blanks, and of the immobile face, recurs in the early poems of *The Colossus* and elsewhere. Five years later, this same nightmarish horror is still evident. This time, Plath is specific about the need to keep writing in order to prevent the onset of what she knows to be an awful, deadly paralysis. If she is not writing, she says, her 'imagination stops, blocks up, chokes me' (*J* 284). The very thing that offers a cure or escape (writing) is thus fundamentally, even fatally, linked with the very thing that threatens her life (the imagination). Later, in July 1958, Plath refers to her paralysis as a 'self-induced vacuum' (*J* 404). The image recalls the central metaphor of *The Bell Jar*. The implication is that Plath, like Esther in the novel, has sucked all of the life-giving air out of her environment, and has thus created the conditions for her own suffocation.

If *Letters Home* represents an attempt to persuade the mother of the stability of Plath's position and of the validity of the decisions she has made, then the *Journals* arguably represent an attempt to persuade and reassure the self. Again, we can trace this interest from the time of the earliest entries through to the final extant journal. In an entry of 15 June 1951, for example, Plath slips into the second-person voice in order to castigate herself. She speaks to herself as a well-meaning mentor or parent might speak to an errant protégée, pointing to the benefits she has had, enumerating her reasons to be cheerful and admonishing herself to take stock, to make something of her life (*J* 64). The self-surveillance becomes a trigger for self-laceration. On 9 February 1958 she observes that the day has disappeared in a 'stupor' (significantly, the day 'spent itself' as though she were a mere passive bystander, again powerless to stem the flow of time). In an attempt to free herself from this stultifying numbness, she inflicts pain on herself – anything, it seems, to break the paralysis: 'fortified by coffee and scalding tea: a series of cleansings' (*J* 327). In May of that year, Plath mentions first her mother, then her husband, and then makes a plea to be left alone, saying that without distractions she will be able to 'flay' herself into some kind of supreme poet (*J* 381). To 'flay' is to strip away the layers or distractions that prevent her commencing the very process. The art, from this point of view, emerges from solitary, violent, self-punishment – a kind of ritualised beating or self-excoriation. An earlier (self-flagellating) letter to the self, dated June–July 1953 – that is, the summer immediately before her suicide attempt – and included as an appendix to the *Journals* begins by excoriating the self as an overindulged baby. This self-critical address is all the more chilling for the studied coolness of its tone. The speaker is not so much angry or despairing, as contemptuous. She catalogues her failings, judiciously weights up the pros and cons of various options, and performs a rigorous cost-benefit analysis of her desires and achievements. In the process, she works her way round to persuading herself of the rightness of a particular action (in this case, not attending Harvard Summer School), though the careful logic of the case she lays out barely masks the contradictory impulses which seem to lie beneath it (*J* 543–6).

Subsequent letters function in similar ways to castigate the self and to urge some particular frame of mind or course of action. An entry of 1 October 1957 is addressed not to the self but to 'a demon'. Here Plath describes the sensation of being double or split; an internal voice calls to her, pointing out all her failures. It is a 'murderous self' which threatens to become indivisible from the speaking or 'good' self (*J* 618, 619). The speaking self must corral all her resources in order to escape this damaging, potentially annihilating other (*J* 620). She assumes a stoical voice and sets herself clear goals (akin to what she elsewhere calls 'mother's "maxims"' (*J* 215)), resolutely siding with the good self which wants to survive (*J* 621). In examples such as this, Plath's *Journals* give us a glimpse of a subjectivity in the laborious process of construction and maintenance. In a fragment of 5 November 1957, for example, written as a note to the self, Plath consciously seeks to make herself into someone different and better. It is 'time to take myself in hand', she says, and to 'build' something new. Step by step, she must prepare a different self to show to her husband, to her class, to her mentors and colleagues (*J* 622–3).

Just as in *Letters Home*, this process carries a price. Plath's self-assessments frequently include a measure of monetary value or, conversely, worthlessness. A long and despairing entry of 19 May 1958 (shortly after Plath had encountered Hughes in what she perceived as an illicit conversation with a female student) laments her loss of faith in her husband and her disappointment with other acquaintances, and calculates these losses in financial terms as though only then can she realise their full value. The rhetoric here is of 'trust funds' and bankruptcy as the full impact of what she sees as dishonesty on the part of the husband is assimilated as the financial ruin of the self (*J* 391). Plath's role mimics that of her mother in *Letters Home*: the investment she has poured into her relationship with her husband is regarded as a sign of trust and a form of contract. Her sense of loss is a measure of her feeling that the trust and investment have been abused. Elsewhere, Plath's apparent failure to achieve 'big returns' (that is, significant financial recompense) for her writing is read as a sign of personal worthlessness (*J* 405).

The self-surveillance I have identified here never lets up. Even in moments of contentment, Plath is at pains to scrutinise the origins and value of that satisfaction and to upbraid herself about better things she might have done (*J* 141). This self-analysis is not, necessarily, unique or pathological. Arguably, it is a symptom of Plath's place in particular historical and ideological circumstances. Cold War McCarthyite culture was characterised by the simultaneous valorisation and penetration of the private sphere. The intimate, the personal, the known-only-to-oneself, became a domain rich with potential – both on the political level (it is in the private, domestic lives of individuals that secret and traitorous communist thoughts might be harboured) and psychologically. Self-analysis (and the analysis of others, such as the mother (*J* 381)), self-healing and self-improvement lay in the hands – indeed were perceived as the patriotic duty – of good Americans. Plath's relentless self-examination, self-diagnosis and self-admonition reflect tendencies in her particular milieu (*J* 538, 569). The private life of the self is not, however, the only concern of the *Journals*. They also talk more broadly about contemporary ideals of femininity and domesticity (*J* 17, 21, 105), about the threat from nuclear or atomic weapons (*J* 32, 46), about the Holocaust (*J* 330), about the Rosenbergs (*J* 541), the environment (*J* 132) and suburbia (*J* 403), among many other contemporary issues. If the *Journals* are to be read as a narrative of a life, they should also be understood as an account of a life lived in a specific and complex context.

Reception

Sylvia Plath's writing has been the subject of a rich proliferation of critiques and approaches. These include readings which identify the work as confessional, those which highlight mythological elements and those which draw on the insights of psychoanalysis. Diverse and changing forms of feminist approach have also been applied fruitfully over the decades, as have readings that emphasise the specific historical circumstances in which Plath lived and wrote. In this final chapter I outline some of the key critical approaches to Plath's writing, and briefly note some new directions in Plath studies. I begin, though, with one of the major – if disputable – ways of accessing Plath's writing: through the many biographical studies which have emerged in the decades since her death.

Biography

Plath has been the subject of five full-length biographies and countless memoirs, sketches and biographical interpretations. One of the reasons for this plethora of biographical accounts might be that each, on its own, seems unsatisfactory and serves only to stimulate or provoke the next. As Jacqueline Rose puts it, 'Plath biographies tend to answer each other, shouting like opponents across a legal gulf, each one insisting that she or he has a greater claim to the truth than the one who went before.'[1] Perhaps, too, there is something specific to Plath's writing that seems to tantalise readers and biographers, inviting them close but then barring the door to any further scrutiny. To an extent,

Ted Hughes's *Birthday Letters* (1998) works in the same way, seeming to disclose new truths about the Plath-Hughes relationship while always withholding more than it tells.

The ethical debates which accompany the genre of biography have been experienced most acutely and contentiously in Plath's case. This is in part because of the nature of her early death and the legacy of children, husband and family she left behind; in part because – as suggested earlier – the work itself seems to invite a certain kind of biographical reading; and in part because of persistent conflicts between commentators (even family members such as Aurelia Plath) and the Plath Estate, controlled until 1991 by Ted Hughes's older sister, Olwyn. Successive biographers and critics have their own stories to tell of their encounters with the copyright holders. Lynda K. Bundtzen even prefaces her 2001 book *The Other Ariel* with a note about her recent membership of the club:

> In writing this preface, I become part of a tradition in Plath scholarship, a member of a group of scholars, biographers and critics who have been discouraged by the executors of the estate of Sylvia Plath . . . from pursuing their research, scholarship, and interpretations. It is a distinguished company, including Jacqueline Rose, Linda Wagner-Martin and Anne Stevenson among others.[2]

Rose's 1991 book *The Haunting of Sylvia Plath* (which insists in its preface that 'This is not a biography') offers a thought-provoking account of the issues relating to writing about Plath. Janet Malcolm's 'meta-biography', *The Silent Woman* (1994), offers the best overview of the contentious history of the field.

The first full-length biography of Plath was Edward Butscher's 1976 *Sylvia Plath: Method and Madness*. As his later essay, 'In Search of Sylvia: An Introduction' (published in his 1977 edited collection, *Sylvia Plath: The Woman and the Work*) explains, Butscher was quick off the mark in researching the book. When he started work, the authorised biographer Lois Ames was already part way through her own research. Her project was never completed, though her initial sketch of Plath, 'Notes Toward a Biography', appeared in Charles Newman's 1970 collection *The Art of Sylvia Plath: A Symposium*. Although at first anxious not to invade Ames's territory, Butscher soon secured access to a number of Plath's friends and family, interviewing her mother, Olwyn Hughes and various others.[3] As the title of Butscher's biography indicates, he seeks a link between Plath's aesthetics and her psychological wellbeing. The result is a strained attempt to diagnose and pathologise Plath, based on the apparent evidence of her own writing and the witness statements of others.

Butscher applies what Susan Van Dyne calls a 'binary logic of true and false selves'.[4] He adopts the epithet 'bitch goddess' as a way of codifying some of the contradictions he perceives in Plath's life and writing, and he works hard to fit his research findings into this frame. Responses to Butscher's work have been mixed. Van Dyne notes that the book has been 'uniformly disparaged by the Estate and other biographers', while also pointing to its 'frequent, detailed analysis of the form of the poems' and the skill and 'carefulness' of its readings.[5] On the other hand, Gary Lane calls the book 'gossipy' and 'oversimplifying' and 'at best cursory in its criticism'.[6] Butscher's early access to key figures in the events of Plath's life should have provided grounds for an insightful reading. However, too often the biographer's interpretations, speculations and judgements cloud the picture. Of Plath's poem 'Widow,' for example, he complains that 'the bile stains the art' – a failure he traces to the simultaneous breakdown of her own marriage. He claims as certain that which can, at best, be speculation ('no doubt a hidden jealousy on Ted Hughes's part' he asserts at one point) and frequently allows the 'bitch goddess' tag to get the better of him: 'Something was nagging at her unconscious, stirring up the dark waters where the bitch goddess had her nest.'[7] Some years after the publication of *Method and Madness*, the book was implicated in a court case brought by Jane Anderson against a recent film version of *The Bell Jar* when, having read Butscher's biography, she identified herself as the model for the character of Joan Gilling. Hughes (acting on behalf of the Estate) was accused of failing in his duty to prevent such biographical interpretations.[8]

Butscher's biography was followed by Linda Wagner-Martin's 1987 *Sylvia Plath: A Biography*. Adopting a broadly feminist approach, and coming from a background deeply immersed in twentieth-century literature, Wagner-Martin offers a wide-ranging account which is attentive to gender and literary contexts. The biography benefits from Wagner-Martin's access to Plath's working drafts, journals and correspondence which had been newly acquired by the Lilly Library and Smith College. For Van Dyne, this is a 'responsible, temperate account' which, while 'never sensational' does not 'pretend to be exhaustive'. Steven Gould Axelrod calls it an 'evenhanded' book and raises the contentious case of the Plath Estate's alleged attempts to curtail interpretation by requiring extensive changes and cuts to be made to Wagner-Martin's original typescript. Olwyn Hughes, speaking for the Estate, referred to Wagner-Martin's 'work-in-progress', and of a review of the book in its final form, as 'invention of a low order or dramatized scraps of fifth-hand gossip'.[9]

Shortly before the publication of *Sylvia Plath: A Biography*, the poet Anne Stevenson (a contemporary of Plath's, now also living in England) began work on her book *Bitter Fame: A Life of Sylvia Plath* (1989). Arguably the most contentious of these biographies, Stevenson's was written with the approval and assistance of the Plath Estate. Malcolm points out how peculiar it is that an account which has openly benefited from access to key participants and the cooperation of the Estate should have been so roundly vilified for such links.[10] Without doubt Stevenson has been able to identify new material and to offer a new perspective on what was already a familiar tale. However, the prized neutrality of the biographer was widely seen to have been compromised by the extent, and particular bent, of the Estate's involvement. The published edition of *Bitter Fame* is prefaced with an 'Author's Note' which reads: 'In writing this biography, I have received a great deal of help from Olwyn Hughes, literary agent to the Estate of Sylvia Plath. Ms. Hughes's contributions to the text have made it almost a work of dual authorship.' As Malcolm explains, the original version of this note, included in advance proof copies, but excised from the final published edition, takes a different slant: 'This biography', it reads 'is the result of a three-year dialogue between the author and Olwyn Hughes . . . Ms. Hughes contributed so liberally to the text that this is in effect a work of joint authorship.'[11] In later accounts of the traumatic experience of writing the biography, Stevenson further explains that the author's note was written by Olwyn herself 'on pain of withdrawing permission for the use of quotations'. Moreover, it seems that Ted Hughes was also involved. As Stevenson puts it, 'He was more responsible for the book than he lets on.'[12]

Van Dyne suggests that the chief failing of *Bitter Fame* is its 'lack of sympathy for the poet, and, more importantly, for the poetry.'[13] However, we might ask whether the value of the important new information she includes (even the contested, because partial, accounts of the couple's friends Dido Merwin, Lucas Myers and Richard Murphy reproduced as appendices) does not outweigh her personal tastes? One might also argue that Stevenson, while not apparently personally sympathetic to Plath's work, nevertheless recognises and defends its aesthetic and cultural value. Her fine reading of 'Ariel', for instance, applauds its 'extraordinary power – every image is grounded in some *thing*, depicted as if with verbal paint'.[14]

The introduction to the second (1999) edition of Paul Alexander's *Rough Magic* (first published in 1991) starts from a similar position to that which Butscher recalls in 'In Search of Sylvia'; that is, with an account of the biographer's intrepid quest for the primary source of knowledge – Plath's mother. As in Henry James's *The Aspern Papers* (1888), the search is carried out by a single-minded protagonist who seems shocked by other people's unwillingness to subordinate themselves to his task. In the preface to the first edition, Alexander cites his demand to Ted Hughes that they should meet and seems surprised by Hughes's (arguably understandable) reluctance so to do. Alexander then follows up with a veiled warning which seems designed to exculpate himself from his subsequent interpretations, and implicitly to pass the blame on to Hughes for his failure to stop them (there are shades here of the Butscher court case mentioned earlier).[15]

Alexander, like the two previous biographers, makes use of the Plath archives. This detailed research is condensed into extensive sections of paraphrase, coupled with moments of what is, surely, pure speculation: 'Already the day was hot, but Sylvia did not think of the heat'; 'Sitting on the bus, Sylvia thought back over the past two months.' Where Stevenson has been accused of lacking sympathy for her subject, Alexander seems to exude too much, imagining himself into her life in a way which pretends to an insight he cannot possibly possess. Moreover, *Rough Magic* assumes a direct and uncomplicated relationship between Plath's emotions and the body of the poems: 'To purge herself,' he writes authoritatively, 'and to better understand her feelings, she wrote another poem'. From the outset, Alexander's reading of Plath's life is shaped by his awareness of her suicide. He claims that he won access to Aurelia by not being like most 'fans' (whom he disparages for being obsessed with suicide), but then proceeds to mention suicide, death and absence numerous times over the following few pages.[16]

Finally, Ronald Hayman's *The Death and Life of Sylvia Plath* appeared in the same year (1991) as the first edition of Alexander's book. He, too, takes the end (the suicide) as the beginning, asserting its importance on the very first page of the foreword. As he goes on to insist, '[i]t's impossible to understand Sylvia Plath's life without understanding the long relationship with death which was eventually consummated in suicide' (the rhetoric, incidentally, implies a kind of seductive masochism on Plath's part). Where Butscher saw Plath as a bitch goddess, Wagner-Martin as a protofeminist, and Stevenson as demanding, selfish and cold, Hayman paints her securely as a victim.[17]

As this overview of Plath biographies indicates, each tells us as much about its author, and about the biographies which went before it, as they do about the supposed subject. Each differs in terms of the events, voices and interpretations they choose to foreground or, conversely, to omit. And each raises fresh questions about the relationship between poet and speaker, between text and reader, and between poet and other parties (friends, family, other writers).

Confessional

Early and influential readings of Plath's work by Al Alvarez, M. L. Rosenthal, C. B. Cox and A. R. Jones, among many others, established the persistent tendency to read her poetry as confessional – as an extremist art characterised by 'compulsive intensity', authenticity of voice, and transparency of language.[18] To read Plath's poetry as 'confessional' in the terms of these early definitions of the mode is to see it as direct, immediate and autobiographical. It is to imagine that it give us unmediated access to the troubled mind of the poet. Clearly, some of Plath's poetry does invite reading from this perspective. However, there are problems with doing so, not least because to read these poems as though they are 'mere conduits to the truth behind them' (to quote Marjorie Perloff) is to do a disservice to the careful artfulness of the poetics.[19] Insights from Plath's *Journals*, letters and worksheets indicate that these poems were diligently drafted and revised. Draft worksheets reproduced in Hughes's *Winter Pollen*, in *Ariel: The Restored Edition*, in Tim Kendall's *Sylvia Plath* and in Van Dyne's *Revising Life* demonstrate that these are not inadvertent outpourings without mediation or manipulation.

Moreover, to read them in this way is to ignore Plath's evident interest throughout her work in the nonexpressive, nonreferential slipperiness of language; its 'brute materiality' as Karen Jackson Ford puts it in her analysis of 'Words heard, by accident, over the phone', its 'fierce potency and oppressive weight, its perniciousness and ineluctability'.[20] Again and again, from 'Stillborn', 'The Manor Garden', and 'Hardcastle Crags' to 'The Courage of Shutting-Up', Plath is interested in the refusal of language to offer any easy catharsis; she is more engaged with the difficulties of telling than with the promise of relief. Nevertheless, this has been an influential reading of Plath, given substance not least by Robert Lowell's introduction to the first US edition of *Ariel* wherein he asserts that 'everything in these poems is personal, confessional, felt'.[21] Of late, a number of critics have demurred from this position, pointing to significant differences both between Plath's work and confession as usually codified, and between Plath's work and that of her peers. Others have sought to reappraise confessional elements in Plath's work within the framework of a revised and rather more theoretically sophisticated model of the mode – one which draws on the insights of Michel Foucault's thought and of recent developments in poststructuralism. From this point of view, confession is a discursive process, one predicated on a particular power relationship between subject and reader. Veronica Forrest-Thomson argues against the naturalising tendencies of confessional readings (that is, their tendency to reduce poetic language to some straightforward translation or assimilation of the real). Of 'Purdah', for instance, she insists on the importance of reading in terms of artifice or construction instead of referentiality or self-revelation: 'Like all true artificers "I" remains enigmatical, presenting only the words on the page.'[22]

Mythology

One of the first full-length studies of Plath's oeuvre, Judith Kroll's *Chapters in a Mythology: The Poetry of Sylvia Plath* (1976) offers a careful and knowledgeable study of mythical elements in Plath's writing. Kroll worked alongside Hughes on preparatory work for the *Collected Poems* and thus had early and privileged access to drafts and other resources. She identifies patterns and relationships across and between poems, drawing particular attention to resonant motifs, symbols, themes and metaphors. But she also looks beneath the surface resemblances and identifies deeper, mythological significations. For Kroll, it is precisely the mythological elements in Plath's poetry which differentiate it from that of her confessional peers:

> Because a mythic system accommodates the personal element, the voice of her poetry is detached from the personal in a sense that it is not in the 'confessional' poets, whose strategy depends partly upon convincing the reader of a lack of such detachment . . . She has a vision which is complete, self-contained, and whole, a vision of a mythic totality, which such poets as Lowell and Sexton do not have.

Chapters in a Mythology usefully traces Plath's and Hughes's background reading and growing interest in Tarot cards, Ouija boards and other occult practices.[23] Although such an approach potentially liberates Plath from the narrow constraints of the personal, it arguably imposes a new set of limitations. As Stan Smith puts it, 'Plath's poems are first and foremost carefully constructed *texts* [his emphasis]. If their meaning cannot be reduced to the conscious intentions of their author, it equally cannot be reduced to spirit-messages from the unconscious, over which the literary talent has no control.'[24]

Sources cited by Kroll include Sir James Frazer's *The Golden Bough* (1922) and Robert Graves's *The White Goddess* (1948). The 'moon-muse' which appears in many of the poems (Kroll cites 'The Detective' and 'Edge' as examples) draws on Graves's analysis of 'White Goddess myths'. Similarly, the bee poems look to his reading of similar myths of rebirth in ancient mythology and, more importantly, Frazer's work on bee myths and associated hierarchies in other ancient traditions. However, it is not only exact correspondences which are important to Kroll. More valuable still are the processes by which Plath transforms immediate observations into her own forms of myth.[25]

Another early reading which focuses on Plath's mythologies is offered by Barnett Guttenberg in his essay 'Plath's Cosmology and the House of Yeats'.[26] Guttenberg traces Plath's self-confessed fascination with W. B. Yeats (we recall her delight at finding a flat to rent in his former London home (*LH* 477)) and identifies in her work a dialectical pattern – based on the polarity of sun and moon – to match Yeats's. Like Kroll's essay, Guttenberg's work is valuable in suggesting specific sources and reference points. For some readers, though, both approaches are rather reductive in their attempt to pin poems to antecedents; the risk is that one privileges minor or chance occurrences and thereby misses rather more suggestive interpretative possibilities. In his reading of 'Candles', for example, Guttenberg suggests some fruitful comparisons with Yeats's poetry, but he does not address other compelling features of the poem. In addition to referencing Yeats, is not the poem also invoking the Jewish practice of lighting a candle for the dead and thereby sanctifying the lost family's memory? Stanza four's rather formal allusion to memories of the Viennese grandmother and to the troubles associated with that time and place (the 'burghers sweated and wept') suggests an altogether different and personally and historically specific frame of reference than Yeats's mythological back-story can provide.

Moreover, the mythological framework which Kroll, Guttenberg and others identify is manifestly a patriarchal framework. It reads certain symbols (the moon, for example) within a gendered framework. It accords a conventional hierarchical value to some symbols over others and it tends to think in terms of rather dubious fixed (to a poststructuralist or postmodernist point of view) binaries. As recent work on Plath (primarily the work of critics such as Elisabeth Bronfen, Bundtzen and Rose) points out, these are precisely the values and binaries that Plath's poetry refutes – or at least wrestles with.

Sandra M. Gilbert poses a pertinent question in her essay ' "A Fine, White Flying Myth": The Life/Work of Sylvia Plath': '*Why* [her emphasis] do so many women writers characteristically work the mythological vein?' Gilbert dismisses what she calls the 'stereotypical explanation' (that is, the assumption that the 'dark, intuitive, Molly Bloomish female unconscious . . . naturally generates images of archetypal power and intensity'). Instead, she suggests that women writers' turn to mythology – to irrational, unreal, highly charged and symbolic representations of self in an imagined realm – masks the absence in women writers of a sure sense of identity and place in the real world. From this point of view, Plath's engagement with mythology and construction of a myth of her own (the myth of the moon-muse or father-God, for example) is a strategy of displacement which reveals, while it attempts to hide, her actual dissociation from her own subjectivity and experience.[27]

Persuasive though this argument is, it risks conflating the poet with the text. Plath's mythological turn is seen as a kind of reaction or response to intolerable real-life circumstances. Gilbert criticises orthodox sentimental readings of women writers' unconscious use of mythology, but she arguably substitutes a model which denies women writers agency and distance on their work. Might it not be that Plath consciously uses mythological tropes as just one of many imaginative and aesthetic strategies? Might we not say that she exposes myth? Instead of passively channelling it – the story of Narcissus, say, or of Philomela, or Electra, or Oedipus – she actively interrogates and modifies it. There is also the risk in all these readings that the search for universal, timeless archetypes overlooks cultural, historical and ideological concerns which are now recognised to run deep in Plath's writing.

Feminist readings

Gilbert's essay, cited above, is one of many to apply feminist approaches to Plath's work. Plath's writing immediately precedes the emergence of what has since been labelled the second wave of feminism. Betty Friedan's influential book *The Feminine Mystique* (1963) was published just months after Plath's death. It records the experiences of her generation and class as they struggled to reconcile their education and aspirations with the limited roles the ideology of the period allowed them. Friedan's description of her own experience as an intelligent and ambitious young woman growing up in mid-century America strikes chords with the account Plath gives throughout her writing. Rejecting the example of their frustrated housewife mothers, young women looked to other potential models:

> The only other kind of women I knew, growing up, were the old-maid high-school teachers; the librarian; the one woman doctor in our town, who cut her hair like a man; and a few of my college professors. None of these women lived in the warm centre of life as I had known it at home. Many had not married or had children. I dreaded being like them . . . I never knew a woman, when I was growing up, who used her mind, played her own part in the world, and also loved, and had children.[28]

It is because Plath's poems and, more explicitly, the novel *The Bell Jar*, give voice to these experiences and frustrations that they have been so fruitfully read as feminist. Voices as various as 'Pursuit', 'Spinster', 'The Disquieting Muses', 'On the Decline of Oracles', 'Electra on Azalea Path', 'Metaphors', 'Poem for a Birthday', 'You're', 'Tulips', 'Three Women', 'Lady Lazarus' and 'Words' talk about desire, oppression, subjectivity, creativity, the family, pregnancy, transgression, children, the body and language. Her writing, from the early stories and *The Colossus* poems, through to the defiant *Ariel* brings female consciousness, female experience, and for some feminist critics a specific female language, into the foreground.

Early feminist criticism addresses not only the detail of Plath's writing, but the larger patriarchal framework of publishing and reviewing within which her work emerges. Chapter 2 has already touched on this, but to give a specific example of the barriers to women's success as writers, we might look at one of the earliest (and male-authored) reviews of Plath's work: 'As a rule the work of women poets is marked by intensity of feeling and fineness of perception rather than by outstanding technical accomplishment. Miss Sylvia Plath is, however, a young American poetess whose work is almost immediately noticeable for the virtuoso qualities of its style.'[29] In reading Plath from a feminist perspective, critics are both addressing the poetry and seeking to liberate women writers from a patriarchal perspective which would stereotype them as poets of emotion rather than skill, and patronise them with the diminutive 'ess' (poetess). Bernard Bergonzi sees Plath as an exception which proves a rule; the first feminist critiques sought to reshape those rules.

Cora Kaplan's introduction to her section on Plath in the 1975 anthology *Salt and Bitter and Good* was one of the first in a rich seam of feminist accounts to emerge in the 1970s and 1980s, even if she does situate herself to the side of contemporary feminist debates. She dismisses the views of 'some women admirers who read the poetry as explicitly feminist [and] have tried blaming real-life fathers and husbands for Sylvia's death', arguing that such an approach is 'seriously misleading' in part because it 'discounts the cultural sources of the poet's malaise' and in part because 'if Sylvia Plath's isolation and early death were an overdose of patriarchy, it was administered by archetypal fathers, husbands and gods, and by the women who collude with them'. For Kaplan, feminism came a little too late for Plath. Nevertheless, as she concludes, her work should not 'be dismissed or disallowed for its blatant, often angry sexual bias'. Plath is a foremother who has 'made it possible for women today to "curse and write"'.[30] Four years later, Gilbert's essay reads Plath in the context both of earlier women writers (Mary Shelley, Jane Austen, the Brontës) and in terms of the mythological and aesthetic forms available to her. Gilbert is particularly interested in Plath's use of the figure of the double, which she reads as a 'liberating' image.[31]

Alicia Ostriker's powerful account, *Stealing the Language: The Emergence of Women's Poetry in America* (1986), has an important place in second-wave feminist critiques. Ostriker's aim is to assess 'the extraordinary tide of poetry by American women in our own time'. She is interested in work which is 'explicitly female in the sense that the writers have chosen to explore experiences central to their sex' and she regards Plath's work as exemplary of these concerns. In a number of able critiques, usefully interspersed with readings of other poets' work, Ostriker teases out the aspects of Plath's writing which give voice to female subjectivity and experience and are amenable to a feminist critique. In Plath's 'In Plaster' and *The Bell Jar*, for example, Ostriker notes the construction of 'perfect external and ugly internal selves' which she reads as evidence of 'the sense that self-division is culturally prescribed, wholeness culturally forbidden, to the woman and the woman poet'. She is particularly engaged by Plath's experience and representation of the female body, looking, for example, at motifs of strangulation, violence and mutilation in 'Medusa', 'Cut', 'Fever 103°' and elsewhere. She also writes eloquently about female representations of resistance and anger, for example in 'Daddy' and 'Lady Lazarus'. Valuable though Ostriker's argument is, her study finds itself unable to free itself from the fact of Plath's death by suicide, which is here read as though it provides the ultimate, inalienable meaning of the work: 'In *Ariel*, the poet "unpeels" herself from her body in poem after poem, lets her body "flake" away . . . She transforms herself from gross matter to "a pure acetylene virgin" rising toward heaven or to dew evaporating in the sunrise – but transcendence always means death.'[32]

At issue in all these accounts is the tendency – seen also in other perspectives – to conflate the life with the art, the speaker with the poet. The allusion in Gilbert's title to the 'Life/Work' is explicit about this, and she draws conclusions about the impossibility of separating the two: 'Finally the violence seeped in, as if leaking from the poems into the life, or, rather, the death.'[33] This conflation is, arguably, a necessary feature of a feminist perspective which, as one of its founding tenets, seeks to refute arbitrary separations between life and art, experience and representation, the private (personal) and public (political). It is, moreover, a tendency which Plath's poetry with its apparent intimacy of address and its narrative of female experiences seems to invite. As Anna Tripp puts it, 'Plath's biography functions as a very strong lure, even for the most post-Barthesian of critics.'[34] Nevertheless, it is an approach which risks becoming essentialist and reductive. In other words, it risks identifying Plath the person so closely with the voice of the poems that the aesthetic, distancing, artful qualities of the work are overridden. Later feminist approaches have been less interested in the detail of Plath's life and in reading her work as evidence of lived oppression than in identifying broader patterns, processes and significations.

From the late 1980s onwards, a feminist critique based on the philosophical, psychoanalytical and poststructuralist positions adopted by French feminist thinkers have proposed new ways of reading Plath's work. The concept of *l'écriture féminine*, which derives from the work of Hélène Cixous, Julia Kristeva and Luce Irigaray, among others, proposes a theory of sexual difference. It suggests that women writers (and indeed some men) challenge or escape the patriarchal 'symbolic order' of language by returning to the realm of the semiotic – a language of the body which exists before the symbolic and allows women a space wholly attuned to the natural rhythms and cycles of their bodies. It is only by turning to the body, according to Cixous, that 'the immense resources of the unconscious [will] spring forth.' From the perspective of French feminism, the language of the symbolic order stultifies women, denying their subjectivity, repressing their desire, and preventing them from coming fully to writing. For Cixous again, 'woman must write herself: must write about women and bring women to writing, from which they have been driven away as violently as from their bodies . . . woman must put herself into the text'.[35]

Irigaray's essay 'This Sex Which is Not One' offers a potentially productive way of thinking about Plath's widely documented interest in the figure of the double. For Irigaray, female desire 'does not speak the same language as men's desire'. Instead of being singular, it is 'diversified' and 'multiple'. 'Within herself,' Irigaray explains, 'she is already two – but not divisible into ones.'[36]

French feminist readings have proved fruitful for Plath scholarship, for example in the work of Jan Montefiore whose 1987 book (recently reissued in a revised edition) *Feminism and Poetry: Language, Experience and Identity in Women's Writing* assesses the poetry of Emily Dickinson, Adrienne Rich and others from this perspective. Liz Yorke, too, in her 1991 book *Impertinent Voices: Subversive Strategies in Contemporary Women's Poetry* uses ideas emerging from French feminist thought in her reading of Plath's use of figurative language and her negotiation and representation of the maternal bond. What is striking in Plath, she argues, is her willingness to 'enter into the fields of "semantic danger" of her own rage, anguish and desire'.[37] However, such views have not been without their dissenters. Alan Sinfield, citing Juliet Mitchell's book *Women: The Longest Revolution* (1984), notes, 'It has been argued, by Julia Kristeva and others, that "the feminine" constitutes an area of carnival that repudiates patriarchy. But, as Juliet Mitchell replies, this validates "just what the patriarchal universe defines as the feminine, the intuitive, the religious, the mystical, the playful, all those things that have been assigned to women".'[38]

Recent work by Rose (primarily in her essay 'Sylvia Plath – Again' in *On Not Being Able to Sleep*), Elisabeth Bronfen and others develops an interest in language, violence and desire. For Bronfen, it is the mutability of the boundaries between these states, and the consequences of this liminality for female subjectivity, which are a key concern. Rose interrogates the place of poetic language in resolving, in so far as is possible, these kinds of tensions. In 'Daddy', for instance, she suggests, 'Something insufferable at the time, to which the only possible response would be an action, has become bearable by making the passage into words.'[39]

Ford's *Gender and the Poetics of Excess* (1997) similarly reads Plath's writing within a continuum which spans Emily Dickinson, Gertrude Stein and Nikki

Giovanni. Plath's poetics of excess permits her first to exceed or surpass, and then to consume or obliterate, the male-dominated aesthetic which shaped, and continued to control, her writing. By embracing excess, not simply as style but as theme, Plath is able to forge a new poetics, thereby 'enabl[ing] her to address and refute not only the words of the dominant culture but her own complicity in words as well'. Like Rose, Ford observes the self-reflexivity of much of Plath's writing, particularly the later works such as the bee poems, which she reads as 'parallel[ing] a career of writing'.[40]

The poet and critic Deryn Rees-Jones's recent essay on Plath in her book *Consorting with Angels: Essays on Modern Women Poets* offers a reading of the gendered poetics of Plath's work which also brings into play psychoanalytical insights and an awareness of historical and ideological contexts. Rees-Jones is helpfully attuned to English influences on Plath, including Edith Sitwell whose 1940 poem 'Still Falls the Rain' she sees as a source for Plath's 'Lullaby'. Rees-Jones, rather like Paula Bennett and Ford, notes the extremity of Plath's writing, her 'violent projection of self into extreme emotional states or positions within the text, which, in its breakdown of the boundaries between the conscious and the unconscious, the rational and irrational, pleasure and pain, has the power to effect a radical transformation of the self'. This emerges in 'explicitly surreal forms' which are influenced in part by Plath's interest in art and more generally read as a response to the specificities of female experience.[41] Like Christina Britzolakis (see below), Rees-Jones notes spectacular or performative elements in Plath's writing. Her primary argument is that 'the establishment of a female writing self must be done with recourse to writers of both sexes. Plath needs literary models of both genders.'[42]

Psychoanalytical approaches

Psychoanalytical approaches to literature have undergone significant changes in the decades since Plath was writing. Early psychoanalytical readings, such as the work of Butscher (mentioned earlier) and David Holbrook in his 1976 book *Sylvia Plath: Poetry and Existence* stand accused of analysing the writer rather than the work. Thus Butscher introduces his 1977 edited collection, *Sylvia Plath: The Woman and the Work*, with a portrait of Plath as 'another violated little girl, another doomed Oedipal victim'. Later, he diagnoses her as 'repressed', or 'depressed', schizophrenic and melancholic.[43] Butscher's theme was first tried out in his 1976 biography, *Method and Madness*, where he diagnosed Plath's 'neurotic fury', her 'father obsession' and 'inner rages', her 'divided personality', narcissism and 'lurking psychosis'. In one particularly problematic reading, he diagnoses Plath as 'narcissistic' on the grounds of the representation of Henry and Elizabeth Minton in 'Sunday at the Mintons'. Butscher's binary paradigm (method *vs.* madness, goddess *vs.* bitch) coupled with the misogyny of some of his interpretations (from his dismissal of some of Plath's female literary influences to his scepticism about the rape scene in *The Bell Jar*) renders his a limited psychoanalytical portrait.[44]

However, in spite of such inauspicious beginnings, a number of critics have used psychoanalytical processes and insights to generate valuable readings of Plath's work. Axelrod's *Sylvia Plath: The Wound and the Cure of Words* 'combines the rhetoric of psychoanalysis with the rhetoric of literary criticism' to offer an evaluation of Plath's writing in its individual detail, in its relationship to known factors in her life and, perhaps most usefully, in its relationship to larger cultural and literary contexts. This turn towards the cultural and historical is one of the most significant features of recent Plath scholarship. Axelrod's book traces the development of certain concerns and voices in Plath's work, suggesting parallels where appropriate between the specificities of Plath's writing and broader psychoanalytical patterns. These include the relationship between the subject and the father, and the subject and the mother, the constitution of that subject in relation to others (or external objects) and to language. Axelrod's closing chapter, 'There are Two of me Now', draws on Sigmund Freud's work on the uncanny, on Jacques Lacan and on Otto Rank's essay on 'The Double' in order to trace patterns of loss, desire and representation in Plath's work and offers a fine reading of self-reflexive motifs of doubling, mirroring and duplicity.[45] For Axelrod, it is the relationship between language and subjectivity which is the proper concern of psychoanalytical criticism, not the presumed pathologies of the author.

Axelrod, Rose, Al Strangeways (in *Sylvia Plath: The Shaping of Shadows*) and Bundtzen (in *Plath's Incarnations*) all offer suggestive and rewarding psychoanalytical readings of the work. They focus on what the writing tells us, not specifically about Plath and her lived experience, but about larger patterns – of desire, loss, anxiety, melancholia, and so on. These readings help us to rethink the apparent authenticity and referentiality of confessional poetry and to understand how complex are the processes of condensation and displacement which shape it. Rose, for example, observes the 'psychic processes' evident in the poems without using them against Plath as a 'case'. More specifically, her book *The Haunting of Sylvia Plath* addresses what the writing cannot tell us – its 'uncertainty' and 'narrative[s] of silence'. It is not 'Plath' that Rose is interested in reading; it is her 'representations'. And the representations themselves should be understood as complex, often contradictory, internally fissured and therefore resistant to any attempt to view them as the route to some singular truth. Readers have no access to the real, lived 'Sylvia Plath'; they have access to the texts and to the 'textual entities' associated with them. From this, Rose postulates that Plath is a 'fantasy'. Reading her in this light allows us to decipher the richness and suggestiveness both of the work and of its place in our culture.[46]

Britzolakis's 1999 book *Sylvia Plath and the Theatre of Mourning* is interested in the complex processes by which gender and subjectivity are acquired, maintained, presented and interpreted. Like Axelrod, she examines Plath's use of motifs of mirroring and the exploration of family relationships, specifically as these emerge in representations of family debt, influence and estrangement. She addresses Plath's evocation of different forms of spectacular femininity, noting that 'amongst the images of women which appear most frequently in Plath's poetry are those of the prostitute, the female performer and the mechanical woman'. She also discusses concepts of negation and melancholia. The thread which links these processes is the tendency towards self-reflexivity noted already. In Britzolakis's account this is specifically turned to the narratives and procedures of psychoanalysis: 'This self-reflexivity continually complicates and interferes with the possibility of a psychoanalytic reading: Plath interrogates psychoanalysis at the very moment when it purports to interrogate her.'

Finally, what distinguishes later psychoanalytical readings, such as Rose's and Britzolakis's, and differentiates them from the work of, say, Butscher is that this recent work offers a way of opening up rather than closing down the text. For Britzolakis, a recognition of the personal and historical circumstances of the writing is valuable, but it does not represent the whole, or only, story: 'While the trauma, loss, and mourning work staged in the writing can never be entirely disentangled from the narrative of her life and death, it none the less exceeds the personalizations of biography.'[47]

History and politics

Stan Smith's 1982 book *Inviolable Voice: History and Twentieth-Century Poetry* opens with the following observation: 'Most poetry seems to function at a level remote from history, where a dissociated mind confronts a landscape innocent of social meaning.' He goes on to argue that this innocence is a deception: 'All poetry, at its deepest levels, is structured by the precise historical experience from which it emerged . . . a writer is always the creature of circumstance.' This understanding sits at the heart of an exciting recent range of readings of Plath's poetry in relation to particular historical, cultural and ideological circumstances. These readings include analyses of the political nuances of Plath's work (Smith, Robin Peel, Sinfield), of its transatlantic resonance (Tracy Brain, Paul Giles), its relation to environmental concerns (Brain) and its consciousness of race (Renée Curry). They also, potentially, encompass feminist and even psychoanalytical concerns which become, in themselves, profoundly historicised perspectives. Smith's reading recognises that although Plath seems 'an intensely private poet' (for example, in 'The Manor Garden'), this privacy is itself constituted in place and in time.[48]

For Sinfield, to read Plath as a political poet is to fight back against readings which emphasise her madness and suicide and turn her into some kind of unique 'case', absorbed in her own trauma and disconnected from the world around. One way, he says, of 'disempowering Plath's politics is to represent her as a mad genius, supersensitive to the general horror of the modern world, inspired by a poetic furor that drove her ever onward to desperate expression and death'. His readings of key *Ariel* poems ('Daddy', 'Lady Lazarus', 'Purdah') demonstrate how profoundly political are their explorations of female subjectivity, violence and power: 'If, as Plath suggests, "Every woman adores a Fascist" it is because there is indeed a continuity between the patriarchal structures that legitimate state violence and violence against women.'[49]

More recently, Deborah Nelson has proposed a reading of Plath which situates her work (and the emergence of the confessional mode of poetry) within the context of Cold War culture. The inseparability of private and public that Smith noted is experienced most acutely, according to Nelson, in postwar American life where privacy is both valorised and disallowed under a regime predicated on containment and exposure. Confessional poetry allows women such as Plath and Anne Sexton a means of 'dismantling domestic ideology through the act of exposure itself, through the self-disclosure of that which should have been the subject of surveillance'.[50] It is a way of exposing and thus resisting the demands of historical and political circumstance: 'Writing autobiographically was . . . not simply an individual aesthetic choice; it was also a political decision.' Such an insight allows new readings of poems such as 'Cut', which, from this perspective, '[c]ondenses a series of twentieth-century conflicts into one image . . . Plath evokes the enemies of World War II, Germany and Japan; obliquely references the Cold War antagonism between the US and the Soviet Union; and recalls the nativist and anti-immigrant ideology of the Ku Klux Klan, best known for its persecution of African Americans.'[51]

Curry reads 'Cut' as a poem whose central event – the accidental slicing of the top of the thumb – forces on the speaker a realisation of her whiteness and thereby her culpability for racial oppression. Her recent book *White Women Writing White* argues for the importance of foregrounding the 'acknowledged or unacknowledged' assumptions about whiteness which underpin Plath's writing. For Curry, Plath's oft-noted articulation of physicality, otherness and power is inextricably woven into a discourse of racial difference. This is exemplified by the emphatic and rigorous deployment in her poetry of a black/white adjectival binary.[52]

Peel also takes as read the significance of the immediate historical context to the development of Plath's oeuvre. He looks in great detail at the circumstances in which particular works were drafted and draws valuable connections between Plath's own reading, writing, viewing and listening. By tracing her awareness of contemporary events, and themes of violence, passivity, anxiety and suffering in the poems, he is able to offer valuable new readings both of obvious poems ('Daddy' or 'Thalidomide') and unexpected ones. 'Crossing the Water', 'Apprehensions' and 'The Rabbit Catcher', for example, might now be read not simply as meditations on Plath's personal situation (her move to England, her relationship with her husband, and so on) but as an exploration of the 'parallels between the suspicion about the exact nature of the Russian presence in Cuba and the suspicions of personal betrayal'. For Peel, this historical understanding provides 'the most neglected piece in this complex jigsaw'.[53]

Brain's scholarship also usefully restores historical and political agency to Plath's work. She draws particular attention to two key aspects of Plath's writing – its transatlanticism (or, as she more accurately defines it, 'midatlanticism') and its deeply rooted concern with the environment. In her essay 'Your Puddle-Jumping Daughter', Brain identifies in Plath's work 'a voice that, like her accent, moved *between* [her emphasis] England and America'. This is a sign of 'perpetual displacement' and evidence of 'a larger crisis about what might constitute European identity'. Most importantly, perhaps, Plath's 'refusal to choose between two places' is symptomatic of a resistance to binary vision in this regard and of the tendency to polarise national and gender identities as 'separate, stable entities'. Like Nelson and Curry, Brain offers a reading of 'Cut' which attends to its historical and ideological significations, specifically as they expose Plath's negotiation of American and European identities in conflict.[54] For Giles, Plath's transatlanticism is best read within the specific context of the 1950s. In these terms, transatlantic exile is an existential and an aesthetic strategy. Giles traces the ways in which national identities are mutually constitutive and mutually sustaining and, in Plath's case, self-consciously constructed and critiqued.[55]

Plath's understanding of environmental and ecological issues is, for Brain, equally important to a full evaluation of the work. She traces the influence on Plath of the new environmental consciousness emerging in 1950s America, represented in particular by the work of Rachel Carson, author of the 1962 book *The Silent Spring* (Plath read some of her earlier work in 1952 and 1958). Anxiety about toxicity, pollution, nuclear fallout and other contaminants can be traced from early unpublished poems such as 'City Wife' to unpublished scrapbooks and is confirmed in new readings of, for example, 'Johnny Panic and the Bible of Dreams', 'The Fifty-Ninth Bear' and 'Elm'. The key insight from this newly discovered environmentalism is that it tells us much about the permeability of boundaries and the liminality of Plath's position as woman and writer.[56]

New directions

What direction will Plath studies take in the years to come? Work by Bronfen, Rees-Jones and others offers refreshingly theorised approaches which read the writing free of the anxiety about biographical reference that has shadowed some earlier critics. Van Dyne, Bundtzen and Brain have established the value of the Plath archive which, as its barriers are slowly loosened, becomes available for attentive new scholarship. Sally Bayley and Kathleen Connors have made the archive the starting point for their research into Plath's broader aesthetic and artistic interests. While some early Plath criticism was interested in the extent of Hughes's influence over her, new work – sustained by Emory University's recent acquisition of the Hughes archive – looks afresh at the nature and direction of that influence. Marsha Bryant has argued for an 'alternative archive for Plath' – one which examines her hitherto overlooked work for a range of popular women's magazines.[57] New research on Plath, for example by Rees-Jones and Thomas Dilworth, scrutinises her engagement with film, and there is much scope for further attention to her relationship with other popular cultural forms (advertising, comic books, radio programmes). Finally, Janet Badia addresses the relationship between Plath and her readers, and examines new mediations of Plath's life and work in contemporary popular culture.

Notes

Preface

1. Marjorie Perloff, 'Sylvia Plath's "Sivvy" Poems: A Portrait of the Poet as Daughter', in Gary Lane (ed.), *Sylvia Plath: New Views on the Poetry* (Baltimore: Johns Hopkins University Press, 1979), p. 173.

1 Life

1. Sandra M. Gilbert, ' "A Fine, White Flying Myth": The Life/Work of Sylvia Plath', in Gilbert and Susan Gubar (eds), *Shakespeare's Sisters: Feminist Essays on Women Poets* (Bloomington: Indiana University Press, 1979), p. 245.
2. Stan Smith, *Inviolable Voice: History and Twentieth-Century Poetry* (Dublin: Gill and Macmillan, 1982), pp. 1–2.
3. Anne Stevenson, *Bitter Fame: A Life of Sylvia Plath* (Harmondsworth: Penguin, 1990), p. 4.
4. Ibid., p. 6.
5. Louis Simpson, *Studies of Dylan Thomas, Allen Ginsberg, Sylvia Plath and Robert Lowell* (London: Macmillan, 1978), p. 91.
6. Ibid., p. 92.
7. See also Rosellen Brown, 'Keeping the Self at Bay', in Paul Alexander (ed.), *Ariel Ascending: Writings About Sylvia Plath* (New York: Harper & Row, 1985), pp. 116–24.
8. Nancy Hunter Steiner, *A Closer Look at Ariel* (London: Faber and Faber, 1974), p. 13.
9. See Gordon Lameyer, 'Sylvia at Smith', in Edward Butscher (ed.), *Sylvia Plath: The Woman and the Work* (New York: Dodd, Mead, 1977), pp. 32–41.
10. Robin Peel, *Writing Back: Sylvia Plath and Cold War Politics* (London: Associated University Presses; Madison: Fairleigh Dickinson University Press, 2002), p. 35.
11. Jane Baltzell Kopp, ' "Gone, Very Gone Youth": Sylvia Plath at Cambridge, 1955–1957', in Butscher (ed.), *The Woman*, p. 76.
12. Laurie Levy, 'Outside the Bell Jar', in Butscher (ed.), *The Woman*, p. 43. See also Gilbert, 'A Fine, White', pp. 246–7.

13. Alex Beam, 'The Mad Poets' Society', in *Atlantic Monthly* (July/August 2001). Available online at www.theatlantic.com/issues/2001/07/beam.htm. Accessed 9 December 2003.
14. See Lameyer, 'Sylvia at Smith', pp. 35–6; Judith Kroll, *Chapters in a Mythology: The Poetry of Sylvia Plath* (New York and London: Harper & Row, 1976), p. 60; and Steven Gould Axelrod, *Sylvia Plath: The Wound and the Cure of Words* (Baltimore: Johns Hopkins University Press, 1992), p. 34.
15. Diane Middlebrook, *Her Husband: Hughes and Plath – A Marriage* (New York: Viking, 2003), p. 16.
16. Dorothea Krook, 'Recollections of Sylvia Plath', in Butscher (ed.), *The Woman*, p. 51.
17. Simpson, *Studies*, pp. 107–8.
18. Middlebrook, *Her Husband*, pp. 5–11.
19. See Kopp, ' "Gone, Very Gone Youth" ', p. 75, and Krook, 'Recollections', p. 55.
20. Kopp, ' "Gone, Very Gone Youth" ', p. 79.
21. Anne Sexton, 'The Bar Fly Ought to Sing', in Steven E. Colburn (ed.), *No Evil Star: Selected Essays, Interviews and Prose* (Ann Arbor: University of Michigan Press, 1985), p. 7. See also Robert Lowell, 'Sylvia Plath's *Ariel*', in *Collected Prose: Robert Lowell*, ed. Robert Giroux (London: Faber and Faber, 1987), pp. 122–5.
22. Middlebrook, *Her Husband*, p. 173.
23. Tracy Brain, 'Dangerous Confessions: Sylvia Plath', in Jo Gill (ed.), *Modern Confessional Writing: New Critical Essays* (London: Routledge, 2006), p. 19.
24. Grace Schulman, 'Sylvia Plath and Yaddo', in Alexander (ed.), *Ariel Ascending*, p. 174.
25. Al Alvarez, *The Savage God* (London: Weidenfeld & Nicolson, 1971), pp. 6–7.
26. Middlebrook, *Her Husband*, pp. 164–5.
27. Ibid., pp. 164–75, 184.
28. Alvarez, *The Savage God*, p. 19.
29. Quoted in Deryn Rees-Jones, *Consorting with Angels: Essays on Modern Women Poets* (Newcastle upon Tyne: Bloodaxe, 2005), p. 119.
30. See LTH 213–14; Stevenson, *Bitter Fame*, 296–7; and Middlebrook, *Her Husband*, 210–11.
31. Gilbert, 'A Fine White,' p. 247.
32. Middlebrook, *Her Husband*, pp. 209–11.

2 Contexts

1. Tracy Brain, *The Other Sylvia Plath* (Harlow: Pearson Education, 2001), p. 46.
2. Pat Macpherson, *Reflecting on The Bell Jar* (London: Routledge, 1991), p. 48.
3. Elisabeth Bronfen, *Sylvia Plath* (Plymouth: Northcote House, 1998), p. 61.
4. T. S. Eliot, *The Sacred Wood* (1920) (London: Faber and Faber, 1997), pp. 45, 47–9.
5. Donald Allen (ed.), *The New American Poetry* (New York: Grove Press, 1960), p. x.

6. Marjorie Perloff, *Poetic License: Essays on Modernist and Postmodernist Lyric* (Illinois: Northwestern University Press, 1990), p. 17.

7. Cleanth Brooks, *The Well Wrought Urn: Studies in the Structure of Poetry* (London: Dennis Dobson, 1949), preface.

8. John Crowe Ransom quoted in Stephen Burt and Jennifer Lewin, 'Poetry and the New Criticism', in Neil Roberts (ed.), *A Companion to Twentieth-Century Poetry* (Oxford: Blackwell, 2001), pp. 154–5.

9. Axelrod, *The Wound*, p. 34.

10. Adrienne Rich, *On Lies, Secrets and Silence: Selected Prose 1966–1978* (London: Virago, 1980), pp. 39–40.

11. Quoted in Kroll, *Chapters*, p. 218, n.11.

12. Stevenson, *Bitter Fame*, pp. 108, 112.

13. Maxine Kumin, *To Make a Prairie: Essays on Poets, Poetry and Country Living* (Ann Arbor: University of Michigan Press, 1979), p. 107.

14. Edward Brunner, *Cold War Poetry* (Urbana and Chicago: University of Illinois Press, 2001), p. xi.

15. Lorrie Goldensohn, *Elizabeth Bishop: The Biography of a Poetry* (New York: Columbia University Press, 1992), p. 63.

16. Axelrod, *The Wound*, p. 126.

17. Karen Jackson Ford, *Gender and the Poetics of Excess: Moments of Brocade* (Jackson: University Press of Mississippi, 1997), p. 13.

18. Patricia C. Willis, *The Complete Prose of Marianne Moore* (London: Faber and Faber, 1987), p. vi.

19. A. R. Jones, 'Necessity and Freedom: The Poetry of Robert Lowell, Sylvia Plath and Anne Sexton', *Critical Quarterly* 7.1 (1965), pp. 11–30 (p. 13).

20. Judith Harris, 'Breaking the Code of Silence: Ideology and Women's Confessional Poetry', in David Graham and Susan Sontag (eds.), *After Confession: Poetry as Autobiography* (St Paul, MN: Gray Wolf Press, 2001), pp. 254–68. See also Brunner, *Cold War Poetry*, pp. 12, 78.

21. Brunner, *Cold War Poetry*, p. xiv.

22. Deborah Nelson, *Pursuing Privacy in Cold War America* (New York: Columbia University Press, 2002), p. xiv.

23. Hugh Brogan, *The Penguin History of the United States of America* (Harmondsworth: Penguin, 1990), pp. 582–6, and Philip Jenkins, *A History of the United States* (Basingstoke: Macmillan, 1997), p. 227.

24. Quoted in Ian Hamilton, *Robert Lowell: A Biography* (London: Faber and Faber, 1983), p. 88.

25. Quoted in Jenkins, *A History*, p. 239.

26. Peel, *Writing Back*, p. 183.

27. Nelson, *Pursuing Privacy*, p. xiv.

28. See William M. Dobriner, *Class in Suburbia* (Englewood Cliffs, NJ: Prentice Hall, 1963), pp. 65, 67, and Elaine Tyler May, *Homeward Bound: American Families in the Cold War Era*, revised edition (New York: Basic Books, 1999), p. 152.

29. Richard E. Gordon et al., *The Split Level Trap* (New York: Bernard Geis, 1960), p. 27.

30. Lori Rotskoff, *Love on the Rocks: Men, Women and Alcohol in Post-World War II America* (Chapel Hill and London: University of North Carolina Press, 2002), p. 7.

31. Betty Friedan, *The Feminine Mystique* (1963) (Harmondsworth: Pelican, 1982), pp. 53, 54.

32. Deborah Nelson, 'Plath, History and Politics', in Jo Gill (ed.), *The Cambridge Companion to Sylvia Plath* (Cambridge: Cambridge University Press, 2006), p. 29.

33. Ruth Schwartz Cowan, *More Work for Mother: The Ironies of Household Technology from the Open Hearth to the Microwave* (New York: Basic Books, 1983), p. 203.

34. Brain, *The Other Sylvia Plath*, p. 55.

35. Al Alvarez, *The New Poetry*, revised edition (Harmondsworth: Penguin, 1966), pp. 23, 32.

3 Early poetry

1. Jacqueline Rose, *The Haunting of Sylvia Plath* (London: Virago, 1991), p. 73.

2. Helen Vendler, *Coming of Age as a Poet* (Cambridge, MA: Harvard University Press, 2003), p. 165 n.1, and Wagner-Martin quoted in ibid.

3. Peter Davison, 'Inhabited by a Cry: The Last Poetry of Sylvia Plath', in Linda Wagner-Martin (ed.), *Sylvia Plath: The Critical Heritage* (London and New York: Routledge, 1988), p. 81.

4. Rose, *The Haunting*, p. 73.

5. Susan Bassnett, *Sylvia Plath: An Introduction to the Poetry*, second edition (Basingstoke: Palgrave Macmillan, 2005), p. 96. See also Toni Saldívar, *Sylvia Plath: Confessing the Fictive Self* (New York: Peter Lang, 1992) for a detailed reading of the Juvenilia.

6. Mary Lynn Broe, *Protean Poetic: The Poetry of Sylvia Plath* (Columbia: University of Missouri Press, 1980), p. 39.

7. Brain, *The Other Sylvia Plath*, p. 54.

8. Middlebrook, *Her Husband*, pp. 19, 10.

9. Axelrod, *The Wound*, p. 195.

10. Bassnett, *An Introduction*, p. 102.

11. Kroll, *Chapters*, p. 249.

12. Stevenson, *Bitter Fame*, p. 213.

13. Diane Middlebrook, 'The Poetry of Sylvia Plath and Ted Hughes: Call and Response', in Gill (ed.), *Cambridge Companion*, p. 159.

14. Quoted in Tim Kendall, *Sylvia Plath: A Critical Study* (London: Faber and Faber, 2001), p. 28.

15. Virginia Woolf, *Moments of Being* (St Albans: Triad, 1978), pp. 83–4.

16. Quoted in Lynda K. Bundtzen, *The Other Ariel* (Amherst: University of Massachusetts Press, 2001), p. 22.

17. Broe, *Protean Poetic*, pp. 78.

18. Axelrod, *The Wound*, p. 63.
19. Vendler, *Coming of Age*, p. 117.
20. Ibid., p. 121.
21. Thomas Dilworth, 'Colossal Influences on Sylvia Plath', *English Language Notes* 40.4 (2003), pp. 77–82 (p. 81).
22. Rees-Jones, *Consorting with Angels*, pp. 105–6.
23. Brain's analysis of collages contained in Plath's art scrapbooks (now held at the Lilly Library) suggests that contemporary publicity for Frigidaire appliances may have inspired the poem. See *The Other Sylvia Plath*, plate 1 and p. 134 n.47.
24. Seamus Heaney, *The Government of the Tongue* (London: Faber and Faber, 1988), p. 149.
25. Sharon Olds, *Strike Sparks: Selected Poems, 1980–2002* (New York: Knopf, 2004).
26. Kroll, *Chapters*, p. 22, and Rees-Jones, *Consorting with Angels*, p. 99.
27. Kroll, *Chapters*, p. 23.
28. Steven Gould Axelrod, 'The Poetry of Sylvia Plath,' in Gill (ed.), *Cambridge Companion*, p. 78.
29. Sigmund Freud, *On Metapsychology; The Theory of Psychoanalysis* (PFL 11), trans. James Strachey, ed. Angela Richards (Harmondsworth: Pelican, 1984), pp. 437–8.
30. Robert Scholes, 'Esther Came Back Like a Retreaded Tire', in Alexander (ed.), *Ariel Ascending*, p. 133.
31. Axelrod, *The Wound*, p. 208.
32. Stevenson, *Bitter Fame*, p. 207.
33. Ibid., p. 213.
34. Axelrod, 'The Poetry', p. 81, and *The Wound*, p. 223.
35. Alicia Ostriker, *Stealing the Language: The Emergence of Women's Poetry in America* (London: Women's Press, 1987), pp. 81, 83, and Linda Wagner-Martin, *Sylvia Plath: A Biography* (London: Sphere, 1990), p. 184.
36. Vendler quoted in Wagner-Martin (ed.), *The Critical Heritage*, p. 13, and Bennett quoted in Claire Brennan, *The Poetry of Sylvia Plath: A Reader's Guide to Essential Criticism* (Cambridge: Icon, 2000), p. 98.
37. Broe, *Protean Poetic*, pp. 117, 120.
38. Marjorie Perloff, 'The Changing Face of Common Intercourse: Talk Poetry, Talk Show, and the Scene of Writing', in Christopher Beach (ed.), *Artifice and Indeterminacy: An Anthology of New Poetics* (Tuscaloosa: University of Alabama Press, 1998), p. 93.
39. Joyce Carol Oates, 'The Death Throes of Romanticism', in Alexander (ed.), *Ariel Ascending*, p. 36.
40. Rose, *The Haunting*, p. 133.

4 *Ariel* and later poetry

1. Ted Hughes, 'The Art of Poetry LXXI', in *Paris Review* 134 (1995), pp. 55–94 (p. 79).

2. Perloff, *Poetic License*, pp. 175–97.

3. Christina Britzolakis, '*Ariel* and Other Poems', in Gill (ed.), *Cambridge Companion*, p. 110.

4. Ibid., p. 109.

5. Middlebrook, 'Call and Response', p. 162.

6. Ovid, *Metamorphoses*, trans. Mary Innes (Harmondsworth: Penguin, 1955), p. 83.

7. Peel, *Writing Back*, pp. 190–4.

8. Bundtzen, *The Other Ariel*, pp. 20–1, and Middlebrook, *Her Husband*, pp. 161–2. See also Ruth Fainlight, 'Jane and Sylvia', for an explanation of the poem's dedication. Available at www.poetrysociety.org/journal/articles/janeandsylvia.html. Accessed 8 August 2007.

9. Simpson, *Studies*, p. 121.

10. Ovid, *Metamorphoses*, p. 43.

11. Britzolakis, '*Ariel* and Other Poems', p. 119.

12. Susan Van Dyne, *Revising Life: Sylvia Plath's Ariel Poems* (Chapel Hill: University of North Carolina Press, 1993), pp. 113, 171.

13. Smith, *Inviolable Voice*, p. 218.

14. George Steiner, 'Dying is an Art', in Charles Newman (ed.), *The Art of Sylvia Plath: A Symposium* (London: Faber and Faber, 1970), pp. 211–12.

15. Rose, *The Haunting*, pp. 144, 145–6.

16. Steiner, 'Dying is an Art', pp. 218, 217. In her BBC interview Plath explains that because of her family background, her interest in this area 'is uniquely intense' (*PS* 169).

17. Irving Howe, 'The Plath Celebration: A Partial Dissent', in Butscher (ed.), *The Woman*, pp. 230, 233.

18. Quoted in Rose, *The Haunting*, p. 205.

19. Quoted in Brennan, *A Reader's Guide*, pp. 73, 75.

20. Rose, *The Haunting*, pp. 207, 230. Antony Easthope dissents from Rose's position in 'Reading the Poetry of Sylvia Plath', *English* 43 (1994), pp. 223–35.

21. Van Dyne, *Revising Life*, p. 176.

22. Ford, *Gender*, p. 164.

23. Christina Britzolakis, *Sylvia Plath and the Theatre of Mourning* (Oxford: Clarendon Press, 1999), p. 166.

24. Brain, *The Other Sylvia Plath*, p. 16.

25. Bundtzen, *The Other Ariel*, pp. 68, 69.

26. Ford, *Gender*, pp. 121–4. Elizabeth Sigmund provides one among many biographical versions of the events behind the poem. See 'Sylvia in Devon: 1962', in Butscher (ed.), *The Woman*, p. 105.

27. Brain, *The Other Sylvia Plath*, p. 24, and Bundtzen, *The Other Ariel*, p. 20.

28. Bassnett, *An Introduction*, p. 99.

29. Smith, *Inviolable Voice*, p. 201.

30. Bundtzen, *The Other Ariel*, p. 194 n.36.

31. Ovid, *Metamorphoses*, pp. 146–52.

32. Geoffrey Hartman, *Beyond Formalism: Literary Essays 1958–1970* (New Haven: Yale University Press, 1970), p. 337.
33. Nelson, 'Plath, History and Politics', p. 33, and Kendall, *A Critical Study*, p. 107.
34. Middlebrook, *Her Husband*, pp. 168–9.
35. Rose, *The Haunting*, pp. 135–43. Rose's reading of this poem was the cause of deep disagreement between her and the Plath Estate.
36. Axelrod, 'The Poetry', p. 86; Bundtzen, *The Other Ariel*, p. 195 and n.42; Middlebrook, 'Call and Response', pp. 164–5.
37. Douglas Cleverdon, 'On *Three Women*', in Newman (ed.), *The Art*, p. 229.
38. Middlebrook, 'Call and Response', p. 164.
39. Marjorie Perloff, 'On the Road to *Ariel*: The "Transitional" Poetry of Sylvia Plath', in Butscher (ed.), *The Woman*, p. 136.
40. May, *Homeward Bound*, pp. 146–7.
41. Marsha Bryant, 'Ariel's Kitchen: Plath, *Ladies Home Journal* and the Domestic Surreal', in Anita Plath Helle (ed.), *The Unravelling Archive: Essays on Sylvia Plath* (Ann Arbor: University of Michigan Press, 2007), p. 279.

5 *The Bell Jar* and *Johnny Panic and the Bible of Dreams*

1. Charles Newman, 'Candor is the Only Wile: The Art of Sylvia Plath', in Newman (ed.), *The Art*, p. 43, and Mary Ellman, '*The Bell Jar*: An American Girlhood', in Newman (ed.), *The Art*, p. 221.
2. Elizabeth Wurtzel, *Bitch: In Praise of Difficult Women* (London: Quartet, 1998), p. 185, and Peel, *Writing Back*, p. 46.
3. Rose, *The Haunting*, p. 177.
4. Middlebrook, *Her Husband*, p. 198, and Stevenson, *Bitter Fame*, p. 255.
5. Peel, *Writing Back*, p. 262 n.39, and Vance Bourjaily, 'Victoria Lucas and Elly Higginbottom', in Alexander (ed.), *Ariel Ascending*, p. 141.
6. Examples of typical reviews are cited in Wagner-Martin (ed.), *The Critical Heritage*, pp. 52–4 and 99–134, and Janet Badia, '*The Bell Jar* and Other Prose', in Gill (ed.), *Cambridge Companion*, pp. 124–38.
7. Middlebrook, *Her Husband*, p. 227.
8. Wurtzel, *Bitch*, pp. 210–11.
9. Quoted in Badia, '*The Bell Jar*', p. 127.
10. Scholes, 'Esther Came Back', pp. 130, 131.
11. Kroll, *Chapters*, pp. 44, 246 n.6, 237 n.8.
12. Peel, *Writing Back*, p. 48, and Middlebrook, *Her Husband*, pp. 152, 127.
13. Kendall, *A Critical Study*, p. 64, and Brain, *The Other Sylvia Plath*, p. 152.
14. Lameyer, 'Sylvia at Smith', p. 144.
15. Wurtzel, *Bitch*, p. 209.
16. Susan R. Bordo, 'The Body and the Reproduction of Femininity: A Feminist Appropriation of Foucault', in Alison M. Jagger and Susan Bordo (eds.),

Gender/Body/Knowledge: Feminist Reconstructions of Being and Knowing (New Brunswick, NJ: Rutgers University Press, 1992), p. 18.

17. Kendall, *A Critical Study*, p. 114.
18. Newman, 'Candor', p. 35.
19. Quoted in Brain, *The Other Sylvia Plath*, p. 153.
20. Nelson, 'Plath, History and Politics', p. 25.
21. Peel, *Writing Back*, p. 261 n.11.
22. Quoted in Macpherson, *Reflecting*, p. 30.
23. Ibid., p. 38.
24. Murray M. Schwartz and Christopher Bollas, 'The Absence at the Center: Sylvia Plath and Suicide', in Lane (ed.), *New Views*, p. 188.
25. Kroll, *Chapters*, p. 127.
26. Aurelia Plath, 'Letter Written in the Actuality of Spring', in Alexander (ed.), *Ariel Ascending*, p. 216.
27. Brain, *The Other Sylvia Plath*, p. 153.
28. For a full account of events surrounding the publication of the novel and the later film version, see Middlebrook, *Her Husband*, pp. 238–9, and Rose, *The Haunting*, pp. 107ff.
29. Quoted in Simpson, *Studies*, p. 105.
30. Bourjaily, 'Victoria Lucas', p. 151.
31. Kroll, *Chapters*, p. 279 n.52.
32. Quoted in Kendall, *A Critical Study*, p. 57.
33. Quoted in Macpherson, *Reflecting*, p. 93.
34. Lynn Spigel, *Welcome to the Dreamhouse: Popular Media and Postwar Suburbs* (Durham, NC: Duke University Press, 2001), p. 34.
35. Rose, *The Haunting*, p. 73.
36. Ibid., p. 167.
37. Ibid., pp. 179–80.
38. Kendall, *A Critical Study*, p. 113.
39. Bronfen, *Sylvia Plath*, p. 76.

6 *Letters Home* and *Journals*

1. Rose, *The Haunting*, p. 75, and Anne Tyler, ' "The Voice Hangs On, Gay, Tremulous"', in Wagner-Martin (ed.), *The Critical Heritage*, p. 211.
2. Middlebrook, *Her Husband*, p. 239.
3. Aurelia Plath, 'Letter Written', pp. 216, 217.
4. Middlebrook, *Her Husband*, p. 239.
5. Perloff, ' "Sivvy" Poems', p. 176. See also Rose, *The Haunting*, pp. 74 and 249 n.38, and Tracy Brain, 'Sylvia Plath's Letters and Journals', in Gill (ed.), *Cambridge Companion*, pp. 139–55, for a discussion of Aurelia Plath's editorial omissions.
6. Janet Altman, *Epistolarity: Approaches to a Form* (Columbus: Ohio State University Press, 1982), p. 2.

7. Rose Kamel, ' "Reach Hag Hands and Haul Me In" ': Matrophobia in the Letters of Sylvia Plath', in Wagner-Martin (ed.), *The Critical Heritage*, p. 223.

8. Erica Jong, 'Letters Focus Exquisite Rage of Sylvia Plath', in Wagner-Martin (ed.), *The Critical Heritage*, p. 208.

9. Robert Giroux, 'Introduction', in Elizabeth Bishop, *One Art* (New York: Farrar, Straus, & Giroux, 1994), p. vii.

10. Tyler, ' "The Voice" ', p. 212, and Carol Bere, '*Letters Home: Correspondence 1950–1963*', in Wagner-Martin (ed.), *The Critical Heritage*, p. 222.

11. Jong, 'Letters Focus', p. 209, and Tyler, ' "The Voice" ', p. 211.

12. Perloff, ' "Sivvy" Poems', p. 156.

13. Britzolakis, *Theatre of Mourning*, p. 22.

14. Michel Foucault, 'Technologies of the Self', in Luther H. Martin et al. (eds.), *Technologies of the Self: A Seminar with Michel Foucault* (London: Tavistock, 1988), pp. 28, 40, 49.

15. Kamel, ' "Reach Hag Hands" ', p. 223, and Axelrod, *The Wound*, p. 95.

16. Perloff, ' "Sivvy" Poems', p. 161.

17. Brain has argued the opposite view: 'A writer as self-consciously ambitious as Plath is likely to have written her journals with a continual fantasy and even occasional conviction that some day they would be read by a larger audience.' See Brain, 'Sylvia Plath's Letters', p. 143.

18. Hughes, 'The Art of Poetry,' p. 71.

19. Brain, *The Other Sylvia Plath*, p. 207.

20. Middlebrook, *Her Husband*, pp. 257–8, 259–61. See also Janet Malcolm, *The Silent Woman: Sylvia Plath and Ted Hughes* (London: Picador, 1994) for a full and fascinating account of the circumstances surrounding the publication of Plath's *Journals*.

21. Middlebrook, *Her Husband*, p. 261, and Malcolm, *The Silent Woman*, pp. 5–6.

22. Miriam Levine, '*The Journals of Sylvia Plath*', in Wagner-Martin (ed.), *The Critical Heritage*, p. 311.

23. Hughes, 'The Art of Poetry,' p. 78.

24. Brain, 'Sylvia Plath's Letters', p. 141.

25. Marni Jackson, 'In Search of the Shape Within', in Wagner-Martin (ed.), *The Critical Heritage*, p. 305.

26. Jacqueline Rose, 'So Many Lives, So Little Time', *Observer*, Review section, 2 April 2000, p. 11.

27. Brain, 'Sylvia Plath's Letters', p. 145.

28. Friedan, *The Feminine Mystique*, p. 67.

7 Reception

1. Jacqueline Rose, *On Not Being Able to Sleep: Psychoanalysis and the Modern World* (London: Chatto & Windus, 2003), p. 51.

2. Bundtzen, *The Other Ariel*, p. ix.

3. Edward Butscher, *Sylvia Plath: Method and Madness* (New York: Seabury Press, 1976), pp. 3–29.
4. Susan Van Dyne, 'The Problem of Biography', in Gill (ed.), *Cambridge Companion*, p. 5.
5. Ibid., p. 7.
6. Lane, *New Views*, p. x.
7. Butscher, *Method and Madness*, pp. 302, 303.
8. Rose, *The Haunting*, pp. 106ff.
9. Van Dyne, 'The Problem', pp. 8, 9; Axelrod, *The Wound*, p. 19; and Olwyn Hughes quoted in Rose, *The Haunting*, p. 93.
10. Malcolm, *The Silent Woman*, p. 12.
11. Quoted in ibid., p. 12.
12. Quoted in Van Dyne, 'The Problem', pp. 10, 11.
13. Ibid., p. 11.
14. Stevenson, *Bitter Fame*, p. 272.
15. Paul Alexander, *Rough Magic: A Biography of Sylvia Plath* (New York: Da Capo Press, 1991), pp. 2–3.
16. Ibid., pp. 282, 194, 230, ix.
17. Ronald Hayman, *The Death and Life of Sylvia Plath* (London: Heinemann, 1991), pp. vii–xiv, 78, 85, 155. As early as 1981, Plath's contemporary and fellow poet Denise Levertov was arguing against this tendency to conflate femininity, creativity and suicide. See Levertov, *Light Up the Cave* (New York: New Directions, 1981).
18. C. B. Cox and A. R. Jones, 'After the Tranquillized Fifties', *Critical Quarterly* 6.2 (1964), pp. 107–22.
19. Perloff, *Poetic License*, p. 51.
20. Ford, *Gender*, p. 128.
21. Lowell, *Collected Prose*, p. 122.
22. Veronica Forrest-Thomson, *Poetic Artifice: A Theory of Twentieth-Century Poetry* (Manchester: Manchester University Press, 1978), p. 163.
23. Kroll, *Chapters*, pp. 87, 3, 41.
24. Smith, *Inviolable Voice*, p. 218.
25. Kroll, *Chapters*, pp. 53, 52, 136–43, 78–9.
26. Barnett Guttenberg, 'Plath's Cosmology and the House of Yeats', in Gary Lane (ed.), *Sylvia Plath: New Views on the Poetry* (Baltimore: Johns Hopkins University Press, 1979), pp. 138–52.
27. Gilbert, ' "A Fine, White"', pp. 248–9.
28. Friedan, *The Feminine Mystique*, pp. 66–7.
29. Bernard Bergonzi, 'The Ransom Note' in Wagner-Martin (ed.), *The Critical Heritage*, p. 32.
30. Cora Kaplan, *Salt and Bitter and Good: Three Centuries of English and American Women Poets* (London: Paddington Press, 1975), pp. 290, 291.
31. Gilbert, ' "A Fine, White"', p. 253.
32. Ostriker, *Stealing the Language*, pp. 7, 83, 100–103, 144, 102.

33. Ibid., p. 247.

34. Anna Tripp, 'The Death of the Author: Sylvia Plath and the Poetry of Resistance', unpublished PhD thesis, University of Wales, Cardiff (1994), p. 20.

35. Hélène Cixous, 'The Laugh of the Medusa', in Elaine Marks and Isabelle de Courtivron (eds.), *New French Feminisms: An Anthology* (Brighton: Harvester, 1981), pp. 250, 245.

36. Luce Irigaray, 'This Sex Which is Not One', in Marks and de Courtivron (eds.), *New French Feminisms*, p. 100.

37. Liz Yorke, *Impertinent Voices: Subversive Strategies in Contemporary Women's Poetry* (London: Routledge 1991), p. 50.

38. Alan Sinfield, *Literature, Politics and Culture in Post-War Britain* (London: Athlone Press, 1997), p. 221.

39. Bronfen, *Sylvia Plath*, pp. 66, 76–89.

40. Ford, *Gender*, pp. 133, 148.

41. Rees-Jones, *Consorting with Angels*, pp. 110–11, 98, 107.

42. Ibid., p. 124.

43. Butscher, *The Woman*, pp. 5, 24, 28, 29.

44. Butscher, *Method and Madness*, pp. 48, 49, 67, 72, 34, 149.

45. Axelrod, *The Wound*, p. 189. See also Pamela J. Annas, *A Disturbance in Mirrors: The Poetry of Sylvia Plath* (Westport, CT: Greenwood Press, 1988) for a reading of Plath's use of mirror images.

46. Rose, *The Haunting*, pp. 4, 221, 5.

47. Britzolakis, *Theatre of Mourning*, pp. 140, 7, 8.

48. Smith, *Inviolable Voice*, pp. 1, 202.

49. Sinfield, *Literature, Politics*, pp. 209, 224.

50. Nelson, *Pursuing Privacy*, p. 77.

51. Nelson, 'Plath, History and Politics', pp. 23, 27.

52. Renée Curry, *White Women Writing White: H. D., Elizabeth Bishop, Sylvia Plath and Whiteness* (Westport, CT: Greenwood Press, 2000), pp. 166, 2, 126–8.

53. Peel, *Writing Back*, pp. 135–7, 169, 190. See also Peel, 'Body, Word and Photograph: Sylvia Plath's Cold War Collage and the Thalidomide Scandal', *Journal of American Studies* 40.1 (2006), pp. 71–95.

54. Tracy Brain, ' "Your Puddle-Jumping Daughter" ', *English* 47 (1998), pp. 17–39 (pp. 17, 19, 21, 33–5).

55. Paul Giles, 'Double Exposure: Sylvia Plath and the Aesthetics of Transnationalism', *Symbiosis* 5.2 (2001), pp. 103–20.

56. Brain, *The Other Sylvia Plath*, pp. 85, 130.

57. Bryant, 'Ariel's Kitchen', p. 270.

Further reading

Primary sources

Plath, Sylvia. *Ariel*. London: Faber and Faber, 1965; New York: Harper & Row, 1966.
—, *Ariel: The Restored Edition*, ed. Frieda Hughes. London: Faber and Faber, 2004.
—, *The Bell Jar*. London: Heinemann, 1963 (under the pseudonym Victoria Lucas); London: Faber and Faber, 1966; New York: Harper & Row, 1971 (as Sylvia Plath).
—, *Collected Poems*, ed. Ted Hughes. London: Faber and Faber; New York: Harper & Row, 1981.
—, *The Colossus and Other Poems*. London: Heinemann, 1960; New York: Knopf, 1962.
—, *Crossing the Water*. London: Faber and Faber; New York: Harper & Row, 1971.
—, *Johnny Panic and the Bible of Dreams*. London: Faber and Faber, 1977; New York: Harper & Row, 1979.
—, *The Journals of Sylvia Plath*, ed. Ted Hughes and Frances McCullough. New York: Dial, 1982 (abridged edition).
—, *The Journals of Sylvia Plath: 1950–1962*, ed. Karen V. Kukil. London: Faber and Faber, 2000. *The Unabridged Journals of Sylvia Plath*. New York: Anchor, 2000.
—, *Letters Home: Correspondence 1950–1963*, ed. Aurelia Plath. New York: Harper & Row, 1975; London: Faber and Faber, 1976.
—, *Winter Trees*. London: Faber and Faber, 1971; New York: Harper & Row, 1972.

Bibliographies

Northouse, Cameron and Thomas P. Walsh. *Sylvia Plath and Anne Sexton: A Reference Guide*. Boston: G. K. Hall, 1974.
Tabor, Stephen. *Sylvia Plath: An Analytical Bibliography*. Westport, CT: Meckler; London: Mansell, 1987.
Meyering, Sheryl. *Sylvia Plath: A Reference Guide, 1973–1988*. Boston: G. K. Hall, 1990.

Secondary sources

Aird, Eileen. *Sylvia Plath: Her Life and Work*. New York: Harper & Row, 1973. Concise survey of individual volumes; predates the publication of *The Journals* and *Letters Home*.

Alexander, Paul. *Ariel Ascending: Writings about Sylvia Plath*. New York: Harper & Row, 1985. Collection of essays and memoirs by, among others, Ted Hughes, Anne Sexton and Elizabeth Hardwick. Includes Aurelia Plath's 'Letter Written in the Actuality of Spring'.

(ed.). *Rough Magic: A Biography of Sylvia Plath*. New York: Viking, 1991. (Revised edition, New York: Da Capo Press, 1999.) Reading of Plath's life and work which makes valuable use of archives and interviews but remains preoccupied with the nature of her death.

Alvarez, Al. *Beyond All This Fiddle: Essays 1955–1967*. London: Allen Lane, 1968. Contains the defining essay on the confessional mode of poetry.

The Savage God: A Study of Suicide. London: Weidenfeld & Nicolson, 1971; New York: Random House, 1972. Includes Alvarez's contentious account of Plath's last days.

Annas, Pamela J. *A Disturbance in Mirrors: The Poetry of Sylvia Plath*. Westport, CT: Greenwood Press, 1988. Perceptive reading of the poetry, focusing on motifs of mirroring and relating these to questions of identity and history.

Axelrod, Steven Gould. *Sylvia Plath: The Wound and the Cure of Words*. Baltimore: Johns Hopkins University Press, 1992. Thorough, engaging and informed reading of the work drawing attention to literary and psychoanalytical contexts.

Bassnett, Susan. *Sylvia Plath: An Introduction to the Poetry*, second edition. Basingstoke and New York: Palgrave Macmillan, 2005. Useful overview; recently updated to suggest connections with Ted Hughes's *Birthday Letters*.

Bennett, Paula. *My Life a Loaded Gun: Dickinson, Plath, Rich and Female Creativity*. Urbana: University of Illinois Press, 1986. Engaging feminist critique of Plath's aesthetics.

Bloom, Harold (ed.). *Modern Critical Views: Sylvia Plath*. New York and Philadelphia: Chelsea House Publishers, 1989. Collection of critical assessments.

Brain, Tracy. *The Other Sylvia Plath*. Harlow: Pearson Education, 2001. Influential rereading of Plath in the light of transatlantic and environmental debates; makes extensive use of archival resources.

Brennan, Claire. *The Poetry of Sylvia Plath: A Reader's Guide to Essential Criticism*. Cambridge: Icon, 2000. Critical compendium of Plath criticism which reproduces and evaluates extracts from a range of scholarly sources.

Britzolakis, Christina. *Sylvia Plath and the Theatre of Mourning*. Oxford: Clarendon Press, 1999. Sophisticated psychoanalytical reading which draws attention to notions of loss, trauma, melancholia and performance.

Broe, Mary Lynn. *Protean Poetic: The Poetry of Sylvia Plath*. London and Columbia: University of Missouri Press, 1980. Careful assessment of the development of Plath's work in terms of key themes and forms.

Bronfen, Elisabeth. *Sylvia Plath* (British Council Writers and their Work series). Plymouth: Northcote House, 1998. Brief but densely argued study which draws on psychoanalytical and poststructuralist theories.

Bundtzen, Lynda K. *Plath's Incarnations: Woman and the Creative Process*. Ann Arbor: University of Michigan Press, 1983. Draws attention to Plath's poetic processes specifically as they encompass the imaginative, the linguistic and the material.

The Other Ariel. Amherst: University of Massachusetts Press, 2001. Published before the publication of *Ariel: The Restored Edition*; traces hitherto hidden associations between the text as originally published and archival drafts.

Butscher, Edward. *Sylvia Plath: Method and Madness*. New York: Seabury Press, 1976. Early biography offering some rudimentary psychoanalytical readings.

(ed.). *Sylvia Plath: The Woman and the Work*. New York: Dodd, Mead, 1977. Collection of early critical views. Includes contributions by teachers and friends from England and the USA, and essays by Marjorie Perloff and Irving Howe.

Connors, Kathleen and Sally Bayley (eds.). *Eye Rhymes: Sylvia Plath's Art of the Visual* (Oxford: Oxford University Press, 2007). Selection of essays focusing on Plath's artistic interests.

Cox, C. B. and A. R. Jones. 'After the Tranquillized Fifties: Notes on Sylvia Plath and James Baldwin'. *Critical Quarterly* 6.2 (1964), 107–22. One of the first critical essays to read Plath in the context of the nascent confessional mode of poetry.

Curry, Renée R. *White Women Writing White: H. D., Elizabeth Bishop, Sylvia Plath and Whiteness*. Westport, CT: Greenwood Press, 2000. Thought-provoking account of representations of whiteness in Plath and other modern white women poets.

Ford, Karen Jackson. *Gender and the Poetics of Excess: Moments of Brocade*. Jackson: University Press of Mississippi, 1997. Original and persuasive reading of the 'aesthetics of excess' in Plath and other contemporary writers.

Gill, Jo (ed.). *The Cambridge Companion to Sylvia Plath*. Cambridge: Cambridge University Press, 2006. Recent collection of original critical essays on Plath's life, work and contexts. Includes contributions by Susan Van Dyne, Deborah Nelson, Lynda K. Bundtzen, Steven Gould Axelrod and Diane Middlebrook, among others.

Helle, Anita (ed.). *The Unravelling Archive: Essays on Sylvia Plath*. Ann Arbor: University of Michigan Press, 2007. New collection of essays on Plath, many drawing on recent archival scholarship.

Hughes, Ted. 'The Art of Poetry LXXI'. *Paris Review* 134 (1995), 54–94. Includes useful comments on Plath's work and on Hughes's role as her editor.

Letters of Ted Hughes, ed. Christopher Reid. London: Faber and Faber, 2007. A selection of Hughes's letters spanning five decades. Includes letters to Sylvia and Aurelia Plath.

'Notes on the Chronological Order of Sylvia Plath's Poems'. *Tri-Quarterly* 7 (1966), 81–8. Valuable overview of the background to key texts.

Winter Pollen: Occasional Prose, ed. William Scammell. London: Faber and Faber, 1994. Reprints important essays on and introductions to Plath's work.

Kaplan, Cora (ed.). *Salt and Bitter and Good: Three Centuries of English and American Women Poets*. London and New York: Paddington Press, 1975. Early anthology setting Plath's writing in the context of a tradition of women's poetry.

Kendall, Tim. *Sylvia Plath: A Critical Study*. London: Faber and Faber, 2001. Thorough and perceptive close readings of Plath's work.

Kroll, Judith. *Chapters in a Mythology: The Poetry of Sylvia Plath*. London and New York: Harper & Row, 1976. Early study emphasising Plath's debt to Robert Graves, Sir James Frazer and others.

Lane, Gary (ed.). *Sylvia Plath: New Views on the Poetry*. Baltimore: Johns Hopkins University Press, 1979. Collection of essays, memoirs and critiques. Includes Marjorie Perloff's essay on the voices of Plath's poems and *Letters Home*.

Lowell, Robert. 'Sylvia Plath's Ariel' (1966). Rpr. in Robert Giroux (ed.), *Collected Prose*. New York: Farrar, Straus & Giroux, 1987. Lowell's original introduction to the 1966 US edition of *Ariel*.

Macpherson, Pat. *Reflecting on The Bell Jar*. London: Routledge, 1991. Excellent survey of the novel; especially good on its structure and relation to contemporary American culture.

Malcolm, Janet. *The Silent Woman: Sylvia Plath and Ted Hughes*. New York: Knopf, 1993; London: Picador, 1994. Indispensable overview of the contested history of Plath biography.

Middlebrook, Diane. *Her Husband: Hughes and Plath – A Marriage*. New York: Viking, 2003. Comprehensive and accessible account of the writing relationship between Plath and Hughes. Makes extensive use of the Hughes archive at Emory University.

Nelson, Deborah. *Pursuing Privacy in Cold War America*. New York: Columbia University Press, 2002. Influential study of Cold War literature and culture.

Newman, Charles (ed.). *The Art of Sylvia Plath: A Symposium*. London: Faber and Faber, 1970; Bloomington: Indiana University Press, 1970. Early and wide-ranging collection of anecdotes and critical responses.

Orr, Peter (ed.). *The Poet Speaks: Interviews with Contemporary Poets* (London: Routledge & Kegan Paul, 1966). Reproduces Plath's 1962 BBC interview.

Ostriker, Alicia. *Stealing the Language: The Emergence of Women's Poetry in America*. Boston: Beacon, 1986; London: Women's Press, 1987.

Important feminist reading of Plath's life, work and significance to the contemporary women's movement.

Peel, Robin. *Writing Back: Sylvia Plath and Cold War Politics.* London: Associated University Presses; Madison: Fairleigh Dickinson University Press, 2002. Close analysis of Plath's engagement with contemporary politics, identifying specific links between historical events and literary texts.

Rees-Jones, Deryn. *Consorting with Angels: Essays on Modern Women Poets.* Tarset, Northumberland: Bloodaxe, 2005. Perceptive reading of Plath's poetics usefully informed by current psychoanalytical, poststructuralist and feminist thought.

Rose, Jacqueline. *The Haunting of Sylvia Plath.* London: Virago, 1991. Influential and sophisticated psychoanalytical reading of Plath's place in contemporary culture.

On Not Being Able to Sleep: Psychoanalysis and the Modern World. London: Chatto & Windus, 2003. Contains later reflections on the process of writing *The Haunting of Sylvia Plath*.

Rosenthal, M. L. *The New Poets: American and British Poetry Since World War II.* New York: Oxford University Press, 1967. Critical survey of mid-century poetry. Defines and critiques the confessional mode.

Saldívar, Toni. *Sylvia Plath: Confessing the Fictive Self.* New York: Peter Lang, 1992. Reads Plath in terms of debates about subjectivity and confession. Has a useful chapter on the Juvenilia.

Smith, Stan. *Inviolable Voice: History and Twentieth-Century Poetry.* Dublin: Gill and Macmillan, 1982. Studies Plath alongside other modern poets and in terms of her engagement with historical and political concerns.

Stevenson, Anne. *Bitter Fame: A Life of Sylvia Plath.* London: Viking; Boston: Houghton Mifflin, 1989. (Paperback edition, Harmondsworth: Penguin, 1990.) Comprehensive biography written with the cooperation of the Estate and consequently provoking much debate about neutrality and influence.

Strangeways, Al. *Sylvia Plath: The Shaping of Shadows.* London: Associated University Press, 1998. Draws together psychoanalytical and political perspectives on Plath's work. Includes useful selected list of Plath's library.

Uroff, Margaret Dickie. *Sylvia Plath and Ted Hughes.* Urbana: University of Illinois Press, 1979. One of the first accounts to read the poetry of Plath and Hughes in terms of its mutual influence.

Van Dyne, Susan. *Revising Life: Sylvia Plath's Ariel Poems.* Chapel Hill: University of North Carolina Press, 1993. Focuses on Plath's repeated revisions of her poetry. Reproduces and studies a selection of Plath's working drafts.

Vendler, Helen Hennessy. *Coming of Age as a Poet: Milton, Keats, Eliot, Plath.* Cambridge, MA: Harvard University Press, 2003. Identifies defining moments in the work of a range of poets.

Wagner-Martin, Linda. *The Bell Jar: A Novel of the Fifties.* New York: Twayne/Macmillan, 1992. Useful critical assessment attuned to contemporary culture and gender politics.

Sylvia Plath: A Biography. New York: Simon & Schuster, 1987; London: Chatto & Windus, 1988. (Paperback edition, London: Sphere, 1990.) Sympathetic, feminist-inflected reading of Plath's life.

(ed.). *Sylvia Plath: The Critical Heritage.* London and New York: Routledge, 1988. Comprehensive collection of reviews and responses covering Plath's oeuvre to the *Collected Poems* and abridged edition of the *Journals.*

Index

146

The Cambridge Introductions to Literature

AUTHORS

Jane Austen Janet Todd

Samuel Beckett Ronan McDonald

Walter Benjamin David Ferris

J. M. Coetzee Dominic Head

Joseph Conrad John Peters

Jacques Derrida Leslie Hill

Emily Dickinson Wendy Martin

George Eliot Nancy Henry

T. S. Eliot John Xiros Cooper

William Faulkner Theresa M. Towner

F. Scott Fitzgerald Kirk Curnutt

Michel Foucault Lisa Downing

Robert Frost Robert Faggen

Nathaniel Hawthorne Leland S. Person

Zora Neale Hurston Lovalerie King

James Joyce Eric Bulson

Herman Melville Kevin J. Hayes

Sylvia Plath Jo Gill

Edgar Allen Poe Benjamin F. Fisher

Ezra Pound Ira Nadel

Jean Rhys Elaine Savory

Shakespeare Emma Smith

Shakespeare's Comedies Penny Gay

Shakespeare's History Plays Warren Chernaik

Shakespeare's Tragedies Janette Dillon

Harriet Beecher Stowe Sarah Robbins

Mark Twain Peter Messent

Virginia Woolf Jane Goldman

W. B. Yeats David Holdeman

Edith Wharton Pamela Knights

Walt Whitman M. Jimmie Killingsworth

TOPICS

The American Short Story Martin Scofield

Creative Writing David Morley

Early English Theatre Janette Dillon

English Theatre, 1660-1900 Peter Thomson

Francophone Literature Patrick Corcoran

Modernism Pericles Lewis

Modern Irish Poetry Justin Quinn

Narrative (second edition) H. Porter Abbott

The Nineteenth-Century American Novel Gregg Crane

Postcolonial Literatures C. L. Innes

Russian Literature Caryl Emerson

The Short Story in English Adrian Hunter

Theatre Historiography Thomas Postlewait

Theatre Studies Christopher Balme

Tragedy Jennifer Wallace